**Anatomy
of the
Ship**

The Battleship
WARSPITE

Anatomy of the Ship

The Battleship
WARSPITE

Ross Watton

Naval Institute Press

Frontispiece: A line and wash drawing by the author, of *Warspite* in 1920.

© Ross Watton 1986

First published in 1986 by
Conway Maritime Press Ltd,
24 Bride Lane, Fleet Street,
London EC4Y 8DR

Designed by Jonathan Doney
Typesetting by Witwell Ltd, Liverpool
Printed and bound in Great Britain by
R J Acford, Chichester

Published and distributed in the United
States of America and Canada by the
Naval Institute Press, Annapolis,
Maryland 21402.

Library of Congress Catalog Card No.
86-61781

ISBN 0-87021-994-4

This edition is authorized for sale only
in the United States and its territories
and possessions, and Canada.

Contents

ACKNOWLEDGEMENTS

I would like to thank all the people that have contributed information and advice, in particular:

Lt Ron Martin RN Rtd, Honorary Secretary of the HMS *Warspite* Association;

Mrs Alma Topen of the University of Glasgow;

Mr Michael Leek;

Mr J Dix;

Mr David Lyon and various other members of staff at the National Maritime Museum, Greenwich.

Finally, I am especially grateful to my brother Earle Watton for his help in collating information.

Introduction

It would be fair to say, that had it not been for the urgent requirement to go one better and ensure the Royal Navy's supremacy, *Warspite* and her four sister ships in the *Queen Elizabeth* class might have gone relatively unnoticed – or at least been regarded as just part of a logical progression in British battleship design. The story begins with the *Dreadnought* of 1906, a revolutionary ship and the realisation of the First Sea Lord, Admiral Sir John Fisher's desire for a super battleship which combined an all big gun armament with high speed. *Dreadnought* heralded the start of a new era in naval history and her name became synonymous with the goliaths of all other navies.

Fisher had set up an advisory body known as the Committee on Designs, his objective being to ensure that ships were designed and constructed (as far as possible) to the Navy's precise requirements. Their first consideration was for a battleship with 12in guns and a speed of 21kts. On 22 February 1905, after only seven weeks of discussion, an agreed design had been reached. Even more astounding than this, the finished ship was ready for trials by October 1906, the only British battleship built in a year and the first with steam turbines. This new machinery meant a great saving in weight and was strongly favoured by Engineer-in-Chief Rear Admiral Durston and the DNC (Director of Naval Construction) Sir Philip Watts.

The next six years brought further developments to the design of dreadnoughts most notably:

Neptune (1908 estimates) the superimposing of after 12in turrets.

Orion class (1909 estimates) the introduction of 13.5in guns in five centreline turrets forward and aft.

King George V class (1910 estimates) director-controlled secondary armament and searchlights.

Iron Duke class (1911 estimates) secondary armament increased to 6in gun and 3in AA guns fitted.

While in his position as DNC, Sir Philip Watts had been responsible for overseeing the designs of all the dreadnoughts. Appropriately the last of his designs, the *Queen Elizabeth* class, can be considered as not only the culmination of his career but arguably the most attractive battleships ever built.

DESIGN

It was originally intended that the battleships of the 1912 programme should be of similar design to the *Iron Duke* class, but before the finished sketches were approved they were rendered obsolete by the knowledge that America and Japan were building 14in gun battleships. Drastic measures had to be taken to keep ahead, and the newly appointed First Lord of the Admiralty, Winston Churchill, advocated an increase in main armament to 15in, though the gun was still only at design stage. Nevertheless, the Director of Naval Ordnance Rear Admiral Moore had so much faith in this untried weapon that he was willing to stake his career on it. So the gamble was taken and enough guns were ordered for the new ships, which now had to be redesigned, to take the weapon.

With the realisation that the 15in shell would provide a heavier punch with less turrets than the standard five 13.5in of the previous ships, it was decided to omit the middle 'Q' turret. This in turn provided extra space for more boilers, which was felt necessary to provide the specified speed of 25kts. This speed was considered an integral requirement, so to help achieve it oil fuel was chosen as the method of propulsion – as opposed to oil and coal as in previous dreadnoughts. This decision was not taken until the final design had been agreed upon by the Admiralty in June 1912, and not without careful consideration. Oil was more efficient than coal, giving equal endurance for less weight, it was also far easier, cleaner and less time consuming to load. Unfortunately, it came from the Middle East; a vulnerable supply, as opposed to coal which was available at home.

Four of these fast battleships were ordered, the original requirement of three battleships and one battlecruiser being considered no longer necessary. With a fifth ship, *Malaya*, generously paid for by the Federated Malay States, building began in late 1912 and early 1913. A further vessel, *Agincourt*, was ordered under the 1914–15 estimates, but was later cancelled at the outbreak of war.

SERVICE HISTORY

Without doubt *Warspite* had one of the most active and successful service histories of any ship in the Royal Navy. She certainly took part in many of the noteworthy engagements of both World Wars, the first of which was the Battle of Jutland in May 1916. *Warspite* as part of the 5th Battle Squadron under Rear Admiral Evan-Thomas, was steaming several miles behind Admiral Beatty's battlecruisers when contact was made with the German battlecruisers under Admiral Hipper, on the afternoon of 31 May 1916.

Hipper's force turned so as to lead the British battlecruisers

Name	Laid down	Launched	Completed	Built
Queen Elizabeth	21 Oct 1912	16 Oct 1913	Jan 1915	Portsmouth
Warspite	31 Oct 1912	26 Nov 1913	Mar 1915	Devonport
Barham	24 Feb 1913	31 Dec 1914	Oct 1915	John Brown
Valiant	31 Jan 1913	4 Nov 1914	Feb 1916	Fairfield
Malaya	20 Oct 1913	18 Mar 1915	Feb 1916	Armstrong

TABLE 2: **PARTICULARS OF WARSPITE, 1915–1919**

Length overall:	639ft 5in
Length waterline:	634ft 6in
Beam:	90ft 6in
Draught:	28ft 9in
Deep displacement:	33,410 tons (as built)
	33,670 tons (1917)
Shaft horsepower:	75,000 (275rpm)
Speed:	24kts
Oil fuel capacity:	3300 tons
Range:	8600nm at 12.5kts

towards the main German fleet. Beatty's force gave hot pursuit and at 3.32pm engaged the German battlecruisers. Meanwhile, the 5th Battle Squadron were trying to close the gap and finally arrived on the scene at 4.19pm. By 4.33pm the main German fleet under Admiral Scheer was sighted, and Beatty ordered a reverse in course – a signal missed by the 5th Battle Squadron owing to distance and poor visibility. When they did eventually turn to follow Beatty, it was almost too late and they came under a hail of fire from the German fleet. *Warspite* received many hits, but continued to fight on. When she turned again to join the stern of the main battle line her steering gear jammed and she found herself turning toward the enemy, and an easy target. She was hit eleven more times whilst turning almost two full circles, before some control was regained and she made her escape. *Warspite* was ordered to return to Rosyth because of the severe damage she had received. The next morning when approaching Rosyth she was narrowly missed by two torpedoes from a German U-boat which she attempted to ram. *Warspite* arrived back at Rosyth later that day, but despite intense damage only 14 of her crew had been killed and 17 injured.

Warspite's next major battle was during the 1939–45 War when she was affectionately known as the 'Old Lady'. This was the Second Battle of Narvik on 13 April 1940 when in company with nine destroyers she entered the Narvik Fjord in order to finish off eight German destroyers surviving from the first battle. Salvoes from *Warspite*'s 15in guns quickly helped to sink all eight, while her Swordfish biplane not only spotted for her guns but also sank a lurking German submarine, which was the first for a Fleet Air Arm aircraft during World War Two.

During the Battle of Crete, on 22 May 1941, whilst in the Kithera Channel, *Warspite* came under heavy air attack and was hit by a 550lb bomb. The resulting damage included the loss of one of the 4in twin mountings, the evacuating of No 3 boiler room and the death of 38 men. This was not the only damage to *Warspite* inflicted from the air during World War Two, for on 16 September 1943, while on bombardment duties off Salerno, she was attacked by twelve Focke-Wolfe 190 fighter-bombers. However, this was merely a diversionary attack to distract *Warspite*, while three radio-controlled glider bombs were launched from their mother aircraft 20,000ft above. They were first sighted at a height of 7000ft, directly above the ship. With credit

to the German controller, the first bomb made a direct hit just behind the funnel and penetrated right through the ship detonating in the double bottom. No 4 boiler room was completely destroyed and the explosion made a large opening in the ship's bottom. Meanwhile, the second bomb, which looked as though it would go wide, changed its line of descent, narrowly missing the ship to starboard exploding in the water by No 5 boiler room. This caused considerable buckling to the inner and outer bottom, and holed the torpedo bulge in this area. The third bomb exploded safely off the starboard quarter. Nevertheless, the first two bombs had resulted in the flooding of five of the six boiler rooms, and a large majority of surrounding compartments. Sufficient steam was provided by No 1 boiler to enable the crippled ship to move slowly, but this also failed, along with most of the electrical power. Assistance finally came to the ship in the form of six tugs which towed the vessel to Malta, where she was made seaworthy before being taken in tow to Gibraltar. She was, however, sufficiently repaired in time to take part in the Normandy landings which were the last major operations of her full career of thirty years.

CAREER SUMMARY

26 November 1913: Launched, Devonport dockyard, by Mrs Austen Chamberlain
8 March 1915: Commissioned by Captain Philpotts
13 April 1915: Joined 5th Battle Squadron, Scapa Flow
16 September 1915: Grounded
17–22 September 1915: Repairs at Rosyth
22 September – 20 November 1915: Repairs at Jarrow
3 December 1915: Collision with *Barham*
11–21 December 1915: Refit at Devonport
31 May 1916: Battle of Jutland
1 June 1916: Docking and repairs at Rosyth
23 July 1916: At Scapa Flow
24 August 1916: Collision with *Valiant*
26 August – 28 September 1916: Repairs at Rosyth
19 December 1916: Captain Philpotts relieved by Captain de Bartolome
11 June 1917: Minor collision with destroyer
7 February 1918: Hoisted Flag of Vice Admiral commanding 5th Battle Squadron

12 March – 6 May 1918: Refit at Rosyth
3 June 1918: Captain de Bartolome relieved by Captain Lynes
21 November 1918: Participated at surrender of German High Seas Fleet, Scapa Flow
1919 – 1924: Atlantic Fleet
1924 – 1926: Refit Portsmouth. First major modifications
1926 – 1930: Mediterranean Fleet
1930 – 1932: Atlantic Fleet
1932 – 1934: Home Fleet
1934 – 1937: Major reconstruction, Portsmouth
29 June 1937: Recommissioned by Captain Crutchley
14 January 1938: Arrived Malta, for Mediterranean Flagship duty, until 6 November 1939
13 April 1940: Second Battle of Narvik
11 May 1940: Hoisted Flag of Admiral Cunningham as C-in-C, Mediterranean Fleet
9 July 1940: Off Calabria engaged Italian battleships
18 August 1940: First bombardment of Bardia
18 December 1940: Bombardment of Vallona
3 January 1941: Bombardment of Bardia
31 January 1941: Accidentally rammed by destroyer *Greyhound*
28 March 1941: Battle of Matapan
21 April 1941: Bombardment of Tripoli
22 May 1941: Seriously damaged by air attack, off Crete
24 May 1941: Alexandria
25 June – 11 August 1941: Passage to USA for repairs
28 December 1941: Repairs completed
February 1942: Joined Eastern Fleet, then to Mediterranean
February 1943: Escorted Australian troop convoy to UK
17 July 1943: Bombardment of Catania
8 September 1943: Escorted surrendered Italian fleet to Malta
11–16 September 1943: Bombardment in support of Salerno landings
16 September 1943: Severely damaged by German glider-bombs, towed to Malta
19 September 1943: Arrived Malta
1–12 November 1943: Towed to Gibraltar
9 March 1944: Sailed for UK
6 June 1944: Operation Neptune: D-Day bombardment
13 June 1944: Damaged by magnetic mine off Harwich. Repaired at Rosyth
25 August 1944: Bombarded Brest
10 September 1944: Bombarded Le Havre
1 November 1944: Supported Walcheren landing
1 February 1945: Paid off into 'C' Category Reserve
31 July 1946: Approved for breaking up
12 March 1947: Towed from Portsmouth for Faslane
23 April 1947: After breaking her tow she ran aground in Prussia Cove, Cornwall. She was sold for scrap and broken up at Mounts Bay over the next nine years.

CONSTRUCTION

The *Queen Elizabeth* class had been designed to a displacement of 31,500 tons (deep load), but all five ships weighed more, *Warspite* particularly at 33,410 tons. By the end of 1917 and post-Jutland improvements, this figure had increased to 33,670 tons, though she was now only third heaviest in the class. The original excess load, is mainly attributed to the additional stiffening required behind the forward side plating of the hull. This was to reduce the strain of heavy pounding when the ship was at speed, or in rough conditions. Extra girders were also arranged under the forecastle deck, to take the massive blast shock of the forward turrets firing.

The increased displacement naturally resulted in a much deeper draught (approximately 34ft); subsequently impairing the speed and seakeeping qualities. There was also the problem of the ship's metacentric height (more than any previous dreadnought); this, coupled with the lower freeboard, made for an unsteady gun platform.

Despite the accrued weight, armour protection was not a strong feature, the old adage of armour thickness matching main armament calibre having been dropped in favour of increased speeds at the beginning of the dreadnought era.

GENERAL ARRANGEMENTS AND HULL STRUCTURE

The hull was built along what was by now conventional lines, employing well established methods of construction. In general the layout was similar to the *Iron Duke* class, the main exception being the absence of 'Q' turret. Instead, the forecastle deck was continued aft to 'X' turret, and in its original configuration, the space between the after funnel and after superstructure was a boat deck. There was no horizontal access through water-tight bulkheads below the middle deck, while entry to original engine rooms and the port side of the boiler rooms was via electric lifts from the main deck. Oil fuel tanks were situated both sides of the engine and boiler rooms and, in the double bottom compartment under the engine rooms. Reserve feed water tanks were under the middle of the boiler rooms, separated from port and starboard double bottom oil fuel compartments by air spaces. Two fresh water tanks, with a combined capacity of 350.9 tons, were sited under the platform deck aft of 'Y' shell room. Another smaller tank (57.6 tons) was on the lower deck forward of 'A' barbette. The general arrangements – save for the engine and boiler rooms – remained little changed throughout the ship's life.

Riveting was employed in all the original construction of the ship, it being the traditional and well accepted method of shipbuilding. Welding was not used until much later, with the bulge plating and the tower superstructure. The double bottom of the ship, which ran the length of the boiler and engine rooms, extended round the bilge up to the outer downward incline of the middle deck. The oil and water tanks in the double bottom, were boundered by oil-tight and water-tight frames, respectively. Between these, bracket and lightened plate frames sub-divided the compartment and were worked between the continuous longitudinal framing of the double bottom.

The transverse frames, forward and aft of the double bottom, were spaced at 4ft intervals, and formed from channel and 'Z' bars. Longitudinal strength was provided by stringers, mid-way between the decks, and worked intercostally with the frames. Floor plates, connected the transverse frames with the ship's keel, while transverse beams were bracketed to the frames. These beams were usually of angle bulb plate, though channel bars were used under areas requiring more strength. Longitudinal 'I' girders and channel bars were fitted between the frames, and the deck plating riveted on top. Vertical strength was provided by stiffened bulkheads and by pillars in larger compartments.

Protection: The side armour was arranged in two tiers, bolted from inboard, against a backing of 3in thick teak planking. The upper part was of 6in thickness, extending from 'A' to 'X' barbette between the upper and main deck levels. The ends were boxed by the 6in thick embrasures shouldering 'Y' barbette, and the 6in to 10in armour round the front of 'A' barbette. The lower armour belt extended to the lower deck and was tapered in section, the upper 4ft increasing from 6in to 13in (the maximum), which continued down 6ft before reducing to 8in over the bottom 3ft. These plates were 15ft wide; however most of the value against shell fire – afforded by the 13in armour – was wasted under water, because of the deep draught. The ends of the main belt were enclosed by 6in transverse bulkheads around 'A' and 'Y' barbettes, on the middle deck and around 'A' barbettes on the lower deck.

The remaining side armour was of 6in and 4in thickness, either end of the lower belt. A pointed 4in collision bulkhead enclosed the forward end of this belt on the middle and lower deck aft of 'Y' turret. The barbette armour was of varying segmented thickness, the greatest (10in) being on the beam above the upper deck; this reduced down to 7in at the centre of the ship and down to 4in on the middle deck. Main machinery, magazine and shell room spaces were further shielded by a box citadel, formed by longitudinal and transverse torpedo bulkheads, from the middle deck to the ship's bottom. These were made from two layers of 1in HT (high-tensile) steel.

Deck armour was an even poorer relation in terms of protection, as it was then thought unlikely that shells would strike the ship from above. This would eventually be proved wrong, with the improvement of aerial bombing and long range shell fire, but unfortunately, as *Warspite* discovered during the Second World War, the progress in these areas was too great for the deck armour she eventually received. In general most decks were little over 1in thick, but it can be argued that horizontal protection was also provided by the *number* of decks.

The Battle of Jutland brought about the first increases to armour protection with the addition of 1in HT steel on the existing middle deck over the main magazines and to the athwartship bulkheads at the outer ends of the magazines. In later warships more protection was given to the magazine by placing it below the shell room. Further improvements came during the large refit of 1924–26, most notably the fitting of external bulges to the ship's side. This was a direct result

TABLE 3: **PARTICULARS OF PROTECTION**

Armour

Main belt:	13in reducing to 6in and 4in forward and aft
Upper belt:	6in
Bulkheads:	6in and 4in forward and aft
Turrets:	11in sides, 13in face
	4.5in roof
Barbettes:	10in to 7in above belt, 6in to 4in below
6in battery:	6in; 2in NC after 1934
Conning tower:	11in sides, 3in roof, 4in revolving hood; altered to 3in NC sided front, 2in NC back, after 1934
Communications tube:	6in to upper deck, 4in below; 4in and 3in respectively after 1934
Torpedo conning tower:	6in
Torpedo conning tower tube:	4in to upper deck

Protective plating (Horizontal)

Forecastle deck:	1in over 6in gun battery
Upper deck:	2in to 1¼in from 'A' to 'Y' barbettes
Main deck:	1¼in at forward and after ends 3⅛in; 1⅞in and 1¼in after 1934
Middle deck:	1in, increased by 1in over magazines after Jutland; after 1934 5in over magazines (4in NC over 1in HT), 3.5in over machinery (2.5in NC over 1in HT)
Lower deck:	3in in extreme ends, 2.5in over steering gears, 1in forward

Protective plating (Vertical)

Torpedo bulkheads:	2in (1in + 1in)
Magazine ends:	2in (1in + 1in), increased by 1in after Jutland
Funnel uptakes:	1.5in

of the Washington Conference of 1921–22, where it had been agreed to allow an increase of 3000 tons to existing capital ships, for the improvement of protection against air and underwater attack.

The Admiralty considered that sub-surface protection was the more important, since money would not be available for both. In actual fact, the deck protection could not have been successfully improved without the fitting of bulges, for reasons of top-weight and stability. However, the fitting of the water-tight bulges almost rectified the overweight condition of the ship. *Warspite* was the first of the *Queen Elizabeth* class to be so fitted. The bulges increased the beam to 104ft, which would only leave eight dry-docks in home waters capable of taking the ship, and none at Devonport. The bulge was of welded construction, consisting of an upper and lower compartment, covering the full depth and length of the main armour belt. It was divided vertically by water-tight bulkheads at 20ft intervals. A step-out below the waterline at the top of the lower compartment, helped to steady the ship, along with the bilge keel, re-instated along the mid-length of the bulge. Protection compartments were also fitted adjacent to the main magazines; these and the double-bottom, could be flooded to give more protection. Likewise, the fuel tanks either side of the main machinery afforded protection and were kept as full as possible, though the double-bottom could also be flooded for extra strength.

Final improvements to protection came in 1934–37, nineteen years after the ship's completion; *Warspite* became the first capital ship to undergo major reconstruction. The main engine and boiler rooms were divided by a centre-line bulkhead and transverse bulkheads, which greatly increased the water-tight integrity and strength of the ship in this region. Horizontal protection was increased on the middle deck, which received 2.5in NC (non-cemented) armour over the main magazines, replacing the post-Jutland 1in HT steel plating.

MACHINERY (see Drawing section C)

Warspite's design speed was 23kts at 56,000shp (shaft horsepower), with a maximum of 25kts, at an overload rate of 75,000shp. During the contractor's trials in 1915, she achieved 24.1kts at 56,580shp and 24.65kts at 75,510shp (overload). Stowage was provided for 3500 tons of oil fuel, though only 2800 tons were normally carried, because of the over-displacement problem. One hundred tons of coal was also shipped in two bunkers below the main deck forward; this was for domestic use.

Steam power was supplied to the turbines at a pressure of 235psi (pounds per square inch), by twenty-four Yarrow large-tube boilers, six per boiler room. The four propeller shafts were coupled to the Parsons direct-drive turbines, operating at a maximum of 275rpm (revolutions per minute). The two inner shafts were each connected to an LP (low pressure) ahead and astern turbine, in the centre engine room. While HP (high pressure) ahead and astern turbines in both wing engine rooms, powered the outer shafts. A reaction-type geared cruising turbine, was attached to the forward end of the HP turbines.

The original main machinery was removed during 1934–37, and replaced by more efficient and lighter equipment weighing 2300 tons (with associated machinery), which meant a saving of 1391 tons. New machinery included six Admiralty three-drum boilers with super-heaters, and four Parsons single-reduction turbines. Each boiler now had its own compartment, while the old forward boiler room was redesigned and fitted with decks to accommodate diesel oil tanks, two dynamo rooms, magazine, high-angle control position and stores. The engine rooms were also sub-divided into gear rooms and turbine rooms, all four units being completely separate. New 12ft propellers were fitted and the shaft horsepower increased by 5000shp to 80,000shp, producing 300rpm, and a speed of 23.5kts; displacement was now 36,450 tons (deep load).

The old Napier screw steering gear that had operated the two rudders was replaced by an electro-hydraulic four-ram unit; but it did nothing to relieve the steering trouble that plagued *Warspite*. At Jutland, the jamming of her helm was through excessive use of wheel at speed; causing over-heating and finally seizing up of the valve gear. With the new equipment the rudders were found to be over-balanced and power was not sufficient to right them after large movements of the wheel. This was partially rectified by removing the front 18in from both rudders, and finally resolved by increasing the relief pressure on the gear from 2000psi to 2400psi. Meanwhile, abnormally high wearing had been found on the inner shafts at the low and high pressure couplings. This was from the interaction of the inner and

TABLE 4: COMPARISONS OF MACHINERY CAPABILITIES BEFORE AND AFTER RECONSTRUCTION

	Before	After
Shp (full power):	75,000	80,000
Rpm (full power):	275	300
Fuel consumption full power (tons per hour):	41	26.8
Endurance at 10kts (nautical miles):	8400	14,300

outer propellers, as the inner propeller passed through the wake of the outer propeller when the ship turned. The problem was surmounted by slowing down the outer shaft on the outside of a turn, whenever more than 5° of wheel was used at speeds over 200rpm.

Auxiliary machinery remained little changed throughout, and consisted of two oil-driven 450kW (kilowatt) dynamos, two turbine-driven 200kW dynamos' supplying a common ring main with 220 volts dc. A fifth 200kW dynamo was added after the First World War.

ACCOMMODATION (see Drawing section D)

Warspite, when first commissioned in 1915, was home for approximately 951 officers and men. As a flagship, large quarters were provided for an admiral, these were situated right aft on the main deck. The captain had a suite of cabins on the starboard side of the upper deck forward of 'X' barbette. Senior officers' cabins were on the upper deck, while most junior officers' cabins were located on the middle deck, aft of 'Y' barbette.

The officers had their meals in the wardroom, opposite the captain's cabin on the port side of the upper deck. The absence of coal bunkers allowed a great saving in space and the provision of numerous washplaces, hammock and kit-locker flats. This made for more pleasant living conditions, especially in the large messdecks on the main deck where there were no portholes. Ventilation was regulated by supply and exhaust fans throughout the ship.

The junior rates meals were cooked (on *coal-fired* ranges) in the ship's galley, on the forecastle deck. These were later changed to oil-fired ranges in 1934. The food was sent to the messes via a lift down to the servery, where it could be despatched to the messes. The crew slept in hammocks slung in the messdecks and other convenient compartments around the ship.

Despite extensive modernisation in 1934 the accommodation arrangements remained relatively unchanged, a condition made worse by an increase in the complement to 1184 men during the Second World War.

ARMAMENT (see Drawing section G)

The main armament: The strength of this class of battleship largely depended on the unproven 15in gun, the ultimate success of which could not have been imagined. It was developed to the low velocity and heavy projectile formula, which reduced the wear on the barrel and increased armour penetration range. The gun was developed under a veil of secrecy, being referred to as the '14in experimental' or, more colloquially, the 'Hush and push' gun. The builders had agreed to have one gun completed for trials in four months.

Loading at the breech could take place at all angles, up to the maximum elevation of 20°; all training, elevation, hoists, loading rammers and breeches were hydraulically powered by four steam pumps, situated either side of the 15in barbettes on the lower deck. The turrets could train at 2° per second and the guns elevate at 5° per second.

The main defects affecting the early performance of this weapon were the inferior armour-piercing shells and flash-tight precautions within the turret and barbette. Both faults were realised as a result of hard lessons learnt at Jutland; measures were taken during the rest of the war to correct them. Flash-tight doors and hoppers were installed on the cordite route from the magazines to the turrets. While an improved hard cap shell was developed, and introduced into service by late 1918. During the 1934–37 reconstruction, the 15in turrets were modernised to take an improved 15in shell and to increase the elevation to 30°.

Secondary armament: *Warspite* was fitted with fourteen 6in guns, two in open mountings on the forecastle deck, and the remainder in casemates round the upper deck. The poor situation of these casemates meant the guns were often awash in rough weather or at speed. To overcome this problem, rubber seals were fitted between the gun shield and ship's side, and 3ft high dwarf bulkheads erected internally to reduce the passage of surface water. Four other 6in guns, were to have been fitted in a similar arrangement on the main deck aft. They were never installed, because as in the *Iron Duke* class, they would have been too low to be of much use.

The port and starboard batteries forward, were supplied with shells by their own separate dredger hoist. Cordite, however, came via Miller's hatches, a slow and unsatisfactory system, which necessitated the stowage of a large number of ready-use charges in the batteries, to keep the guns supplied. During the Battle of Jutland, both *Warspite* and *Malaya* were hit by shells that detonated in the starboard battery, causing Cordite fires and, in *Malaya*'s case, severe casualties and the near loss of the ship. Therefore Miller's hatches were replaced by dredger hoists, and the unloading place on the upper deck enclosed by a handing room.

The after- and foremost guns, along with the 6in armour, were removed during 1934–37, and the casemates rebuilt to 1.5in thickness. The after 6in embrasures on the main deck remained as extra protection for the magazines, though the ship's side was plated over to the upper deck. All the 6in guns were removed during 1944 and the batteries utilised for extra accommodation.

Anti-aircraft armament: At the outset of her career the need for AA defence was minimal and only two 3in AA guns were installed, on the forecastle deck. During 1924–26, these and the two 6in open mountings were replaced by 4in Mk III HA guns. The greatest increase to AA armament came during 1934–37, with the removal of existing AA guns, and the fitting of four 4in Mk XIX twin mountings, four 8-barrelled 2pdr pom-pom mountings and four 0.5in quadruple machine-gun mountings. Further changes to the light AA armament occurred during the Second World War and are covered in table 5.

Torpedo armament: The two submerged torpedo rooms were situated on the platform deck, one forward of 'A' magazine, and the other behind 'Y' magazine. Each contained two 21in torpedo tubes (one to port and one to starboard). Twenty torpedoes were carried, each with a 280lb wet gun-cotton charge, and a maximum range of 18,500yds at 19kts.

FIRE CONTROL ARRANGEMENTS (see Drawing secion H)

Main armament: As built, the 15in guns were controlled from an armoured revolving hood, situated atop an armoured conning tower directly aft of 'B' turret. This hood also contained a 15ft rangefinder and one of two tripod-type direction sights, the other sight being installed in the director tower on the spotting top along with a 9ft rangefinder. Initially all turrets had a 15ft rangefinder but in 1919 30ft rangefinders were fitted to 'B' and 'X' turrets. An open director sight was also provided in each turret for local control. The entire main armament could be controlled from 'B' turret. In 1924, the 15in director tower was resited on a platform below the foretop.

A new 15in director control tower was fitted on the upper bridge during the 1934–36 refit; this was provided with a 15ft rangefinder, and the original armoured hood was moved to the after superstructure. During the latter half of 1941, whilst in the USA, Type 284 radar was added to the 15in director, subsequently being replaced by Type 274 in 1944.

Secondary armament: The 6in control positions were sited abreast the conning tower, secondary director towers being located one either side of the compass platform. These directors were to remain with the ship throughout her life, eventually being moved to either side of the admiral's bridge when the new tower structure was added in 1934–36.

High-angle directors: In 1924–26 a new fore top was fitted to the ship with a HACP (High-angle control position) and Type 'UB4' 12ft rangefinder, for control of the 4in HA guns. In 1931 this system was replaced by HACS Mk I also with a 12ft rangefinder. During the 1934–36 refit the HACS Mk II directors were added to the after part of the Admiral's bridge. Type 285 radar was installed in these directors during 1941.

Mk I** pom-pom directors were sited on the tower superstructure in 1934–36 and were subsequently fitted with Type 282 radar. Two pom-pom directors were also mounted on sponsons on the after superstructure.

AIRCRAFT ARRANGEMENTS (see Drawing section L)

Flying-off platforms were first fitted on top of 'B' and 'X' turrets during 1918. The aircraft carried were a Sopwith 1½-Strutter forward and a Sopwith 2F1 Camel on the after turret. To facilitate take-off the

TABLE 5: SUMMARY OF ARMAMENT

Main armament: 8-15 Mk I, in four twin Mk I mountings (modified Mk IN in 1934)
Secondary armament: 14 – 6in Mk XII, twelve in single P IX mountings and two open mountings (two open mountings removed 1924, four P IX mountings removed 1934, all removed 1944)
Saluting guns: 4 – 3pdr Mk I (in peacetime)
Other guns: 5 – maxim machine guns (in peacetime)
8 – .6 pdr sub-calibre for 15in guns (provided in 1924)
6 – 3 pdr sub-calibre for 6in guns (provided in 1924)
Torpedo tubes: 4 – 21in submerged tubes (after tubes removed 1924, forward tubes removed 1934)
AA armament:

	4in	4in	3in	2pdr	20mm	20mm	0.5in
Gun Mk	V	XVI	I	VIII	IV	IV	III
Mounting Mk	III	XIX	II	VI	V	III	II
Type of mounting	single	twin	single	8-barrel	twin	single	quad
1915	–	–	2	–	–	–	–
1927	4	–	–	–	–	–	–
1937	–	4	–	4	–	–	4
1941	–	4	–	4	–	15	–
1942	–	4	–	4	–	19	–
1943	–	4	–	4	–	35	–
1944	–	4	–	4	4	31	–
1945	–	4	–	4	4	31	–

TABLE 6: PARTICULARS OF GUNS

15in BL Mk I

Calibre:	15in
Length of bore:	42 calibres (630in)
Length of gun:	650.4in
Weight of gun:	100 tons
Weight of shell:	1920lb (4crh)
Weight of cordite (MD45 full charge):	428lb
Muzzle energy:	79,890ft-tons (4crh)
Muzzle velocity:	2450fs (4crh)
Rifling:	Polygroove plain section, MK I, 76 grooves
Length of rifling:	516.33in
Twist of rifling:	Uniform right-hand, 1 turn in 30 calibres
Mounting:	Twin Mk I (modified Mk I N after 1934)
Revolving weight:	750 tons, 815 tons after 1934
Rate of fire:	2rpm per gun
Maximum elevation:	20°, 30° after 1934
Maximum range:	23,734yds (4crh shell), 32,200yds (6crh shell) after 1934
Shell stowage:	773 APC shellite, 40 HE (after turrets), 24 shrapnel (forward turrets), 64 practice

6in BL Mk XII wire-wound (1914)

Calibre:	6in
Length of bore:	45 calibres (270in)
Length of gun:	280in
Weight of gun:	6 tons 14cwt 56lb
Rifling:	Plain section, 36 grooves
Twist of rifling:	Uniform right-hand twist, 1 turn in 30 calibres
Length of rifling:	230.56in
Weight of shell:	100lb
Weight of charge:	28lb 4oz Cordite MD19, later reduced to 27lb 2oz
Muzzle velocity:	2940fs (later 2825fs)
Muzzle energy:	5998ft-tons (reduced to 5530ft-tons)
Mounting:	P IX
Rate of fire:	7rpm
Maximum elevation:	15°
Maximum range:	13,500yds (4crh shell)
Shell stowage:	150 rounds per gun, 100 starshell per ship

4in QF Mk V

Calibre:	4in
Length of bore:	45 calibres (180in)
Length of gun:	187.8in
Weight of gun:	2 tons 1 cwt 38lb
Weight of breech mechanism:	lcwt 64lb
Rifling:	Polygroove plain section, 32 grooves
Twist of rifling:	Uniform right-hand twist, 1 turn in 30 calibres
Length of rifling:	149.725in
Weight of shell:	31lb
Weight of charge:	7lb 11oz Cordite MD16
Muzzle velocity:	3000fs
Muzzle energy:	1930ft-tons
Mounting:	Mk III HA
Rate of fire:	14rpm (at 50°)
Maximum elevation:	85°
Maximum range:	28,750ft (ceiling at 80°)
Weight of mounting excluding gun:	4 tons 12cwt
Shell stowage:	150 rounds per gun, 100 starshell per ship

4 in QF Mk XVI

Calibre:	4in
Length of bore:	45 calibres (180in)
Weight of gun:	2 tons lcwt 11lb
Rifling:	Plain section, 32 grooves
Twist of Rifling:	Uniform right-hand twist, 1 turn in 30 calibres
Weight of shell:	35lb 14oz
Weight of charge:	9lb SC Cordite
Muzzle velocity:	2650fs
Muzzle energy:	1934ft-tons
Mounting:	Twin HA/LA Mk XIX
Weight of mounting (including guns):	16 tons 11cwt
Rate of fire (maximum):	20rpm per gun
Maximum elevation:	80°
Maximum depression:	10°
Maximum range:	21,300yds at 45°; 40,000ft ceiling at 80°
Shell stowage:	2000 HE per ship, 250 starshell per ship

3in BL Mk 1 QF

Calibre:	3in
Length of bore:	45 calibres (135in)
Length of gun:	143in
Weight of gun including breech mechanism:	1 ton
Rifling:	Polygroove plain section, 20 grooves
Twist of rifling:	Uniform right-hand twist, 1 turn in 30 calibres
Length of rifling:	117.5in
Weight of shell:	12lb 8oz
Weight of charge:	2lb 8oz
Muzzle velocity:	2517fs
Muzzle energy:	586ft-tons
Mounting:	Single open Mk II HA
Weight of mounting (excluding guns):	1 ton 16cwt 38lb
Rate of fire:	29rpm
Maximum elevation:	90°
Maximum depression:	10°
Maximum range:	11,200yds at 45°

Vickers 0.5in Mk III machine-gun

Calibre:	0.5in
Length of bore:	62 calibres (31.11in)
Weight of gun:	56lb (62lb with waterjacket full)
Length of gun:	52in
Weight of bullet:	1.32oz
Muzzle velocity:	2520fs
Rate of fire:	600rpm (700rpm maximum)
Maximum effective range:	800yds
Mounting:	Quadruple Mk II
Weight of mounting including guns:	1 ton 5cwt 88lb
Maximum elevation:	80°
Maximum depression:	10°
Shell stowage:	2500 rounds per gun

2pdr QF Mk VIII pom-pom

Calibre:	40mm (1.575in)
Length of bore:	40 calibres (62in)
Length of gun:	102.6in
Weight of gun:	600lb approx
Weight of shell:	2lb
Rifling:	12 grooves
Length of rifling:	54.84in
Twist of rifling:	Uniform right-hand twist, 1 turn in 30 calibres
Muzzle velocity:	1920fs, (2400fs with high velocity shell)
Maximum surface range:	3800yds
Maximum effective range:	1700yds
Rate of fire:	90rpm (115rpm maximum)
Mounting:	8-barrelled Mk VI
Weight of mounting (remote power control and 1200 rounds)	17 tons 7cwt with RPC
Maximum elevation:	80°
Maximum depression:	10°
Shell stowage:	750 rounds per gun

20mm Mk II Oerlikon cannon

Calibre:	20mm (0.787in)
Length of bore:	65 calibres
Weight of gun and mechanism:	150lb approx
Weight of shell:	0.27lb
Weight of cartridge:	0.18lb
Weight of charge:	27.7 grams
Muzzle velocity:	2725fs
Rate of fire:	450rpm
Maximum altitude range:	10,000ft at 87° elevation
Maximum effective range:	1000yds
Maximum surface range:	4800yds at 35° and 6250yds at 45°
Mounting:	Single hand-operated; Mk V twin power-operated
Weight of mounting including gun:	1695lb (1 ton 1 cwt 70lb twin mounting)
Weight of shield:	250lb
Thickness of shield:	0.5in
Maximum elevation:	87° (70° twin mounting)
Maximum depression:	5° (10° twin mounting)

platform was extended over the barrels and supported by angle-bar struts, while the turrets themselves were turned into wind. These aircraft were mainly carried for reconnaisance purposes and to spot for the 15in guns.

However, the use of such aircraft was abandoned until 1934 when a DIIH steam catapult was installed, flush with the forecastle deck amidships. Two large hangars were provided abaft the funnel, along with two 10-ton seaplane cranes for retrieving the aircraft. The original flight consisted of four Blackburn Shark TSR seaplanes, but these were replaced by the Fairey Swordfish MkI before the war. In 1940 the Supermarine Walrus amphibian was carried, but by mid-1943 all aircraft were removed and the hangars used for recreational purposes.

EXTERNAL ALTERATIONS
1916: Main topmast removed and the upper yardarm repositioned across the starfish platform; an ensign gaff was removed from the foremast and W/T aerial outriggers were fitted to the forward arms of the starfish platform and two signal yards angled aft were attached to either side of the spotting top. A small platform was placed on the fore topmast just over the 15in director. An aerial trunk was added just to starboard of the conning tower on the shelter deck. The ensign gaff was repositioned several feet below the mainmast tower platform.

1917: A range clock platform was fitted on the foremast below the spotting top. The fog sirens were resited on an enlarged lower platform to the rear of the mainmast struts. The searchlight control position on the compass platform was enclosed and heightened while the searchlight platform on the after funnel was heightened and a range clock was added to the starboard side. The deckhouse on the port side of the after funnel was enlarged. Rangefinder baffles were temporarily rigged.

1918: A searchlight platform was erected on the after superstructure and another on the rear of the mainmast with a hooded control position above. Training scales were painted on 'B' and 'X' turrets. A short stump topmast was housed on the mainmast platform for the rigging of W/T aerials. The plating on the after 6in embrasures was made flush. Further range clocks were fitted (two either side of the after funnel searchlight tower), while the range clock platform was removed from the fore mast and two range clocks on a pole were arranged just ahead of the foremast. Finally, flying-off platforms were fitted to 'B' and 'X' turret roofs.

1919: The fore topmast was removed, while a topmast with an upper W/T yard was fitted to the mainmast. Two extra searchlight towers were added, one either side of the after funnel. The two vent exhausts from the middle engine room and both sides of the mainmast were heightened; 30ft rangefinders were fitted to 'B' and 'X' turrets. Paravane equipment was installed; this included two derricks positioned over the sounding boom, port and starboard of the forward shelter deck.

1920: The spotting top was enlarged to accommodate high-angle control positions and on top an extra director with 12ft rangefinder. A main topgallant mast with upper W/T yard was fitted and the ensign gaff repositioned onto the mainmast platform. The searchlights were removed from the after superstructure and mainmast platforms. An admiral's stern-walk was fitted. The flying-off platform supports fixed to the 'B' and 'X' turret's barrels were removed, and two range clocks were added on 'X' turret. Two 32ft life-cutters were permanently stowed on radial davits abaft the after funnel. Byers anchors were adopted as the bower anchor port and starboard.

1926: During the large refit of November 1924 – April 1926 (Portsmouth) torpedo bulges were fitted and the after torpedo tubes removed. The forward funnel was trunked into the after funnel. The forward superstructure was modified – the compass platform was enlarged and fitted with steel screens and the admiral's platform and searchlight platforms were also enlarged. The two 36in searchlights were replaced by two 24in signal projectors. The flag deck was extended aft to the base of the trunked funnel, night gun look-out positions were removed and a torpedo control sight with rangefinder positioned on the charthouse. The original 15in director was refitted on a new platform below the spotting top, which was also altered to accommodate a 12ft UB4 rangefinder in a HACP. Outriggers were connected to all the arms of the foremast starfish, and a short stump mast was positioned to the rear of the spotting top to take the W/T aerials. The searchlight platform and control positions were removed from the after superstructure and mainmast. Crossed yardarms were arranged on the mainmast starfish platform, along with a Type 75 short range W/T unit. An admiral's flag pole and larger W/T yard were fitted to the mainmast. Short range fire-control aerials were installed on the after searchlight tower and all range clocks were removed, except for the two on 'X' turret. The fog sirens were repositioned onto the funnel and the aerial trunk on the starboard side of the conning tower moved to the port side. Small oil fuel tanks were fitted, one to port and two to starboard of the boat deck.

1931: High-angle control system (HACS) Mk I was fitted on the spotting top, the small stump mast was removed, and a derrick was

Anchor	Type	Weight	Cable	Remarks
Bowers	Wasteney-Smith stockless	150cwt	3in 500 fathoms each	Replaced by Byers anchor during 1920.
Sheet	Wasteney-Smith stockless	150cwt		Replaced by Byers anchor during 1942
Kedge	Admiralty pattern	5cwt		Two carried amidship. Replaced by two Hall stockless in 1934

rigged between the foremost two 6in guns in the forecastle deck. A Type 75 short range W/T unit was fitted at the rear of the spotting top. The port red flag on the mainmast helm signal was replaced by red 'eggtimer' cones.

1937: March 1934 – March 1937 Major Reconstruction (Portsmouth): *Warspite* emerged from this refit almost a completely different ship. A new gas-tight tower bridge superstructure was fitted, along with new gunnery control equipment, which included a 15in director control tower and two 4in high-angle control towers. A new foremast, mainmast and funnel were installed, as well as a midship catapult and two hangars. Four 4in twin HA mountings and four 8-barrelled pom-poms made up the air defence, augmented by two quadruple 0.5 machine-gun mountings on both 'B' and 'X' turrets. The new boats were now housed on the hangar roof, where they could be hoisted and lowered by the two 10-ton seaplane cranes. The after superstructure was heightened and fitted with a pom-pom director sponson and the original forward 15in DCT. The 6in gun battery was remodelled and the forward and after mountings were removed from each side and the after embrasures were almost concealed behind new side plating. The midship boat boom was resited just forward of the 6in gun battery breakwater.

1942: June – December 1941 refit (USA): during this refit the bridge superstructure was modified, the signal platform was extended aft and the admiral's bridge widened and the foremost part enclosed at the sides. The pom-pom director sponsons either side of the compass platform were enlarged to accommodate further air defence positions. Type 271 surface search radar (later replaced by Type 273) was installed in a lantern on the foremast starfish platform, and the fore topmast was repositioned abaft the mast. Type 281 air search radar was fitted on the fore and main topmasts, with the transmitting office abaft No 2 bridge platform on the starboard side. Two Type 284 surface gunnery radar were fitted on the main DCT, and Type 285 aerials on the HACS directors with offices aft on the admiral's bridge. A Type FM2 medium frequency direction-finding array was installed on the bridge front. Steel screens were fitted outboard of the 4in HA twin mountings and the 32ft life-cutter davits were removed. Surface look-out positions were placed abreast the funnel and the outboard compartments beneath the pom-pom sponsons heightened. The 0.5in machine guns were replaced by Oerlikons, also positioned in sponsons about the ship. The ship was painted with disruptive camouflage.

The Photographs

3. A view of the after turrets and plated-over 6in embrasures taken during docking and repairs after Jutland. Note the shell hit on 'X' turret and patches over the sidelights.

Imperial War Museum

4. At Rosyth during 1918 with heightened searchlight platform on the after funnel and mainmast searchlight platforms fitted.

Imperial War Museum.

5. During 1918 the flying-off platforms were fitted to 'B' and 'X' turrets. This photograph shows the new fore top, additional searchlight towers either side of the after funnel, range clocks, the main topmast with W/T yard, and stern gallery.

National Maritime Museum

6. An excellent photograph of *Warspite* at anchor, probably at Portland.

National Maritime Museum

7. Entering Portsmouth for refit during March 1931: torpedo bulges have been fitted, the forward funnel trunked and the bridge superstructure enlarged. She is also flying a paying-off pennant.

Michael Leek

8. A close-up of the bridge superstructure 1928: the fore top carries a stump mast and a 12ft UB4 rangefinder, which is just visible in this picture.

Maritime Photo Library

9. *Warspite* in July 1931: she has now been fitted with HACS Mk1 on the fore top.

Michael Leek

10. A good close-up of *Warspite*.

National Maritime Museum

11, 12. Two photographs of *Warspite* at anchor, probably at Portland during 1934.

Maritime Photo Library

13. *Warspite* emerging from her major refit for engine trials during 1937. Note the absence of 15in DCT and all the AA armament.

Wright & Logan

14, 15, 16. Three good close-ups of *Warspite* arriving at Malta in January 1938 for Mediterranean Flagship duties.

Wright & Logan

14

15

16

18. Another 1942 shot, taken while refuelling off the Seychelles.
Ronald Martin

17. *Warspite* in 1942 sporting her first camouflage pattern.

Imperial War Museum

19. The Supermarine Walrus is hoisted aboard while anchored off the Maldive Islands. The ships in the background are *Formidable, Mauritius, Lightning* and the auxiliary *Appleleaf*.

Ronald Martin

20, 21. Two pictures showing the embarkation of 15in shells.

Ronald Martin

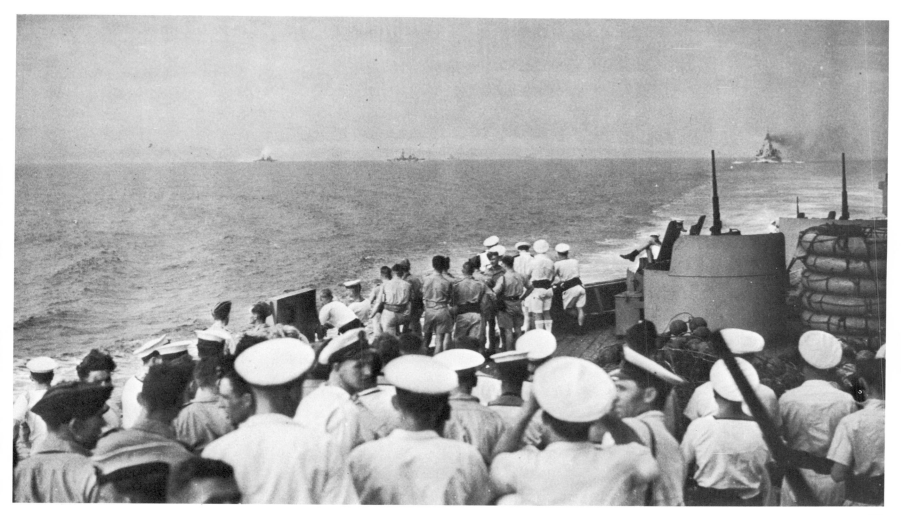

22, 23. These photographs show the placing of Oerlikon mountings around the after superstructure. The first is during the surrender of the Italian fleet, September 1943 and shows two single Oerlikons; the second, taken during the Normandy landings in 1944, shows two twin Oerlikon mountings in the top left corner plus two of the single Oerlikons mounted on the catapult deck.

Mr J Dix

22

23

24. *Warspite* leaving Portsmouth for the scrapyard, a journey she did not complete.

Wright & Logan

25. Being towed into Malta on 19 September 1943 for repairs following a German glider bomb attack. Note how low she sits in the water owing to severe onboard flooding.

Imperial War Museum

26. A line and wash drawing by the author
of *Warspite* in 1937.

The Drawings

A General arrangements

A1 EXTERNAL PROFILE 1917 (all
drawings in section A 1/450 scale)

A1

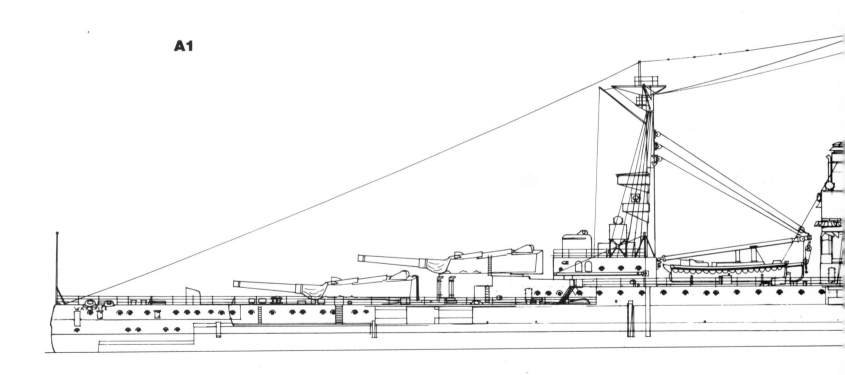

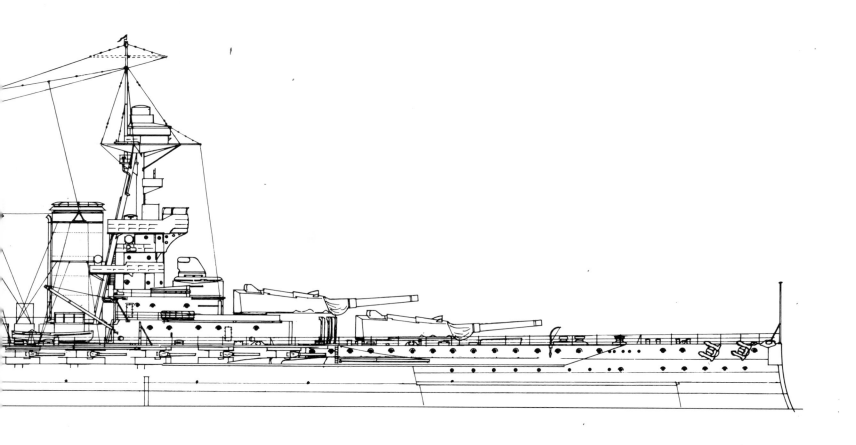

A General arrangements

A2/1

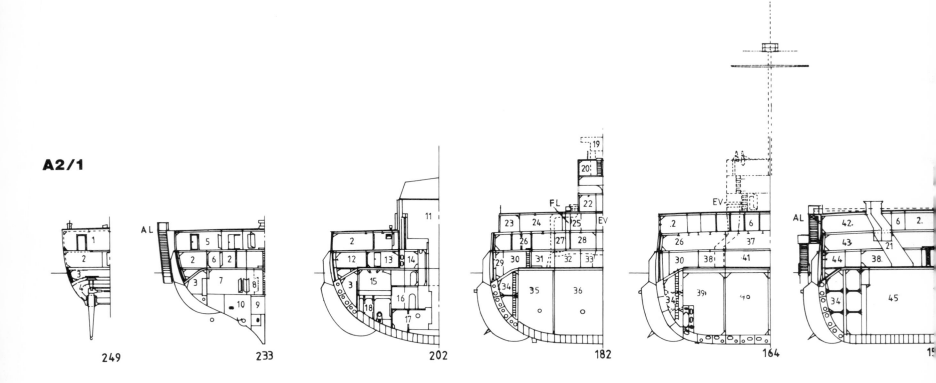

249   233   202   182   164   1

52	No 3 boiler room	65	Central stores	79	Spare alternator room	93	Oar stowage
53	15in director tower	66	Engineer's store	80	Book stall	94	Clothing store
54	Captain's shelter	67	Sub-calibre and small arms store	81	POs' pantry	95	Flour store
55	Charthouse	68	Bomb room	82	Gunnery equipment store	96	No 6 cordage store
56	HF/DF (high frequency direction-finding) office	69	No 3 dynamo room	83	Provision room	97	Electrical store
57	WC	70	Diesel oil fuel tank	84	15in transmitting station	98	CPOs' WCs
58	Captain's bathroom	71	Cypher office	85	Torpedo gunner's store	99	Cells
59	Midshipmen's study	72	RDF office (Type 282 radar)	86	Upper pom-pom magazine	100	Capstan engine room
60	General reading room	73	Gunner's instructional store	87	Lower pom-pom magazine		
61	Ship's galley	74	Ready-use flour store	88	POs' mess	AL	Accommodation ladder
62	Bakery	75	Bread cooling room	89	CPOs' washplace	EV	Exhaust vent
63	6in BL gun space	76	Servery	90	CO_2 machinery compartment	FL	Food lift
64	Main W/T transmitter room	77	High-angle control place	91	Sick bay		
		78	POs' washplace	92	Isolation ward		

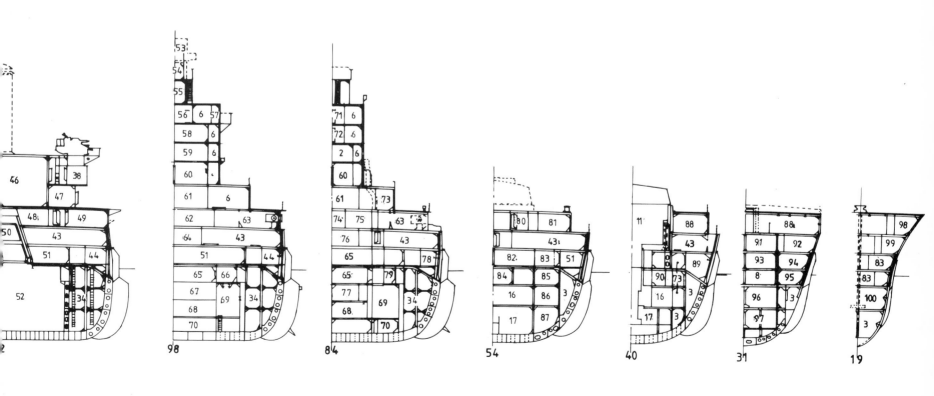

A General arrangements

A2/2 Internal profile 1942

1 Admiral's day cabin
2 Admiral's dining cabin
3 Lobby
4 Staff office
5 Officer's cabin
6 Flooding valve space
7 Central communication office
8 Admiral's and officers', stewards' and cooks' mess
9 Cinematograph store
10 Boiler room vent
11 Stokers' mess
12 Funnel uptakes
13 No 1 W/T transmitter room
14 Servery
15 Boys' mess
16 Dispensary
17 Sick Bay
18 CPOs' mess
19 Cable locker
20 Printing office
21 Boatswain's store
22 Petrol working space
23 Paint room
24 Paint store
25 Writers' main office
26 Outbound correspondence office
27 After capstan flat
28 Ordnance artificers' ready-use store
29 Main machinery and engineers' workshop
30 Stokers' hammock and kit-locker room
31 Searchlight gear stowage
32 RDF office (Type 285 radar)
33 Oil fuel working space
34 Central store
35 Medical distributing centre
36 RDF office (Type 284 radar)
37 Shipwright's workshop
38 Provision room
39 Canvas and cordage store
40 Water-tight compartment
41 Lower paint room
42 Captain's store
43 Awning stowage
44 Blank saluting magazine
45 Small arms magazine
46 Centre gear room
47 Centre turbine room
48 Boiler room
49 Lower steering position
50 Switchboard room
51 15in transmitting station
52 Secondary armament clock room
53 Paravane store
54 Fresh water tank
55 Steering gear compartment
56 Pyrotechnic magazine
57 15in shell room
58 15in magazine
59 15in handing room
60 Air space
61 Silent compartment
62 No 2 W/T transmitter room

A2/2

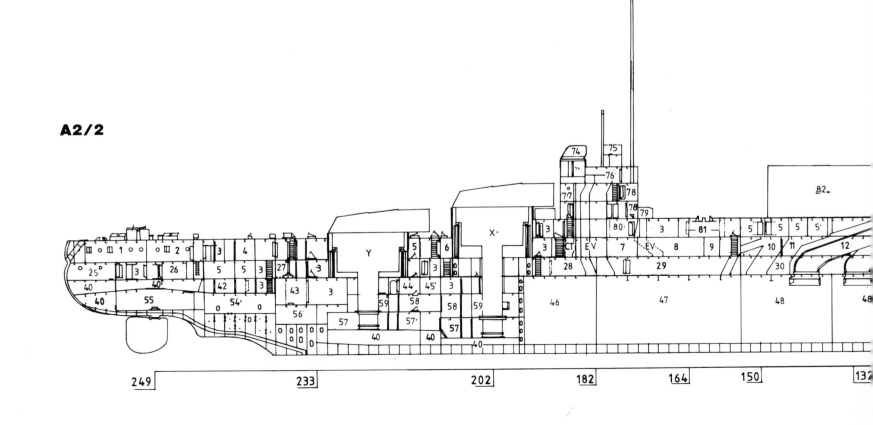

63	Telephone exchange	78	WCs
64	4in HA magazine	79	Catapult control compartment
65	Cool room	80	RDF office (Type 282 radar)
66	Refrigerating machinery compartment	81	Catapult mechanism compartment
67	Capstan engine room	82	Hangar
68	Petrol tank compartment	83	Bakery
69	Engineer's spare gear store	84	Ready-use flour store
70	6in magazine	85	Seamen's heads
71	Diesel oil tank	86	Boys' heads
72	6in shell room	87	Bow compartment
73	Canteen store	88	RDF office (Type 271 radar)
74	15in control tower	89	Charthouse
75	2pdr pom-pom control tower	90	RDF office (Type 285 radar)
76	Aircraft spares stowage	91	Captain's sea cabin
77	15in control tower hand training compartment	92	Remote control office
		93	Plotting office
		94	Admiral's charthouse

95	Signal house	a	Upper bridge and compass platform
96	Signal officer's cabin	b	Admiral's bridge
97	Cypher office	c	Conning tower and signalling platform
98	Conning tower	d	No 2 platform
99	Chief of staff's sea cabin	e	No 1 platform
100	Staff officer's cabin	f	Shelter deck
101	Navigating officer's cabin	g	Forecastle deck
102	Galley vent	h	Upper deck
103	CPOs' recreation room	i	Main deck
104	General reading room	j	Middle deck
105	Oilskin store	k	Lower deck
106	Ship's galley	l	Platform deck
107	Main kitchen	m	Hold
108	Soda fountain bar		

AT	Aerial trunk
CT	Cable trunk
EV	Exhaust vent
FL	Food lift
A	'A' 15in barbette
B	'B' 15in barbette
X	'X' 15in barbette
Y	'Y' 15in barbette

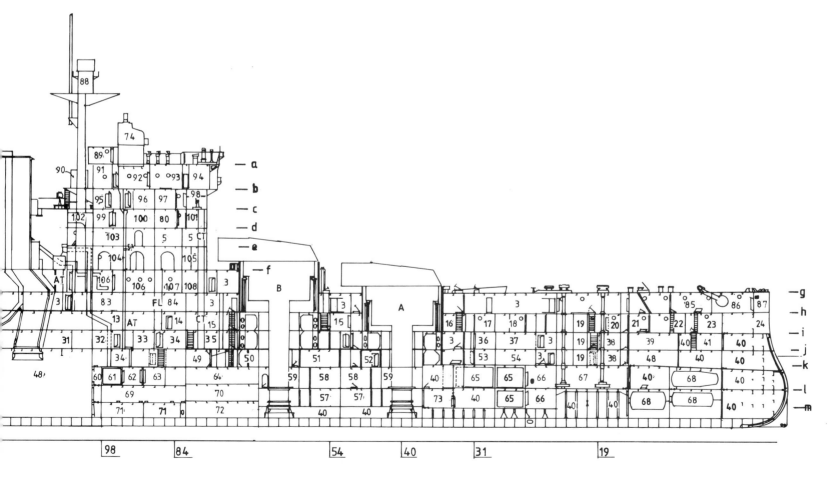

A General arrangements

A3 SUPERSTRUCTURE DECKS

A3/1 No 2 Platform (aft)

1 15in control tower
2 Incendiary locker
3 Pom-pom control tower
4 Emergency control position
5 Crane stowage

A3/2 No 1 Platform (aft)

1 15in control tower support
2 Aircraft store
3 Parachute and clothing store
4 W/T office

A3/3 No 1 Platform (forward)

1 Balsa raft
2 Oil fender and accommodation ladder stowage
3 Oil fender and 20ft motor boat stowage
4 2pdr pom-pom mounting
5 45ft motor boat
6 45ft motor launch
7 35ft motor boat
8 Boiler room vent
9 18in aerial trunk
10 CPOs' recreation room
11 Midshipmen's study
12 Officer's cabin
13 Communication tube

CF Carley float
CT Cable trunk
GV Galley vent

A3/4 No 2 Platform (forward)

1 RDF office (Type 281 radar)
2 Chief of staff's sea cabin
3 Staff officer's cabin
4 Admiral's sea cabin
5 Captain's bathroom
6 Admiral's bathroom
7 RDF office (Type 282 radar)
8 D/F (direction-finding) office
9 Navigating officer's cabin
10 Communication tube

A3/5 Searchlight, conning tower and signalling platforms

1 44in searchlight
2 10in signalling projector
3 20in signalling projector
4 36in searchlight
5 WC
6 Submarine look-out
7 Signalman's shelter
8 Signal house
9 RDF office (Type 284 radar)
10 Signal officer's cabin
11 Cypher officer
12 Conning tower

CT Cable trunk
FL Flag locker

A3/6 Upper platform

A3/7 Admiral's bridge

1 RDF office (Type 285 radar)
2 4in high-angle control tower
3 6in control tower
4 Captain's sea cabin
5 Remote control office
6 Plotting office
7 Admiral's shelter
8 Admiral's charthouse
9 Rangefinder
10 Admiral's conning position
11 6in control position

A3/8 Upper bridge and compass platform

1 Captain's shelter and charthouse
2 15in control tower
3 Air defence look-out position
4 Searchlight sight
5 Target bearing indicator starshell sight

A3/9 Shelter deck

1 Oerlikon positions
2 15in control tower hand-training position
3 Aircraft spares store
4 Gunroom and warrant officers' WCs
5 RDF office (Type 281 radar)
6 10-ton seaplane crane
7 Hangar
8 2pdr pom-pom ready-use magazine
9 2pdr pom-pom support
10 Working platform
11 Meteorological office
12 Incinerator compartment
13 Boiler room vent
14 Beef screen

A3/1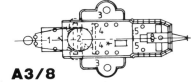

A3/2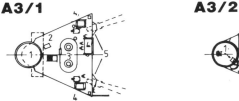

A3/3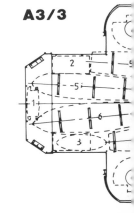

A3/8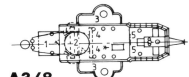

A3/7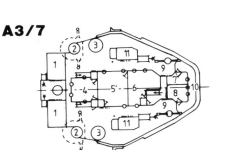

A3/9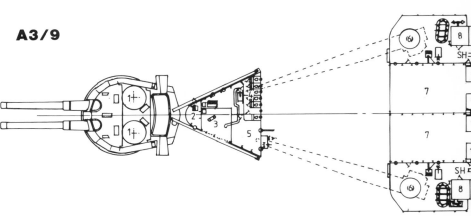

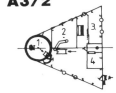

15 Vegetable locker
16 Disinfector compartment
17 Commander's store
18 Welding generator compartment
19 Steel plate rack
20 Surface lookout position
21 Galley flue
22 Boiler room vent
23 General reading room
24 Gunner's ready-use store
25 Searchlight cupboard
26 Oilskin store
27 Communication tube

AT Aerial trunk
GV Galley vent
SH Shell hoist

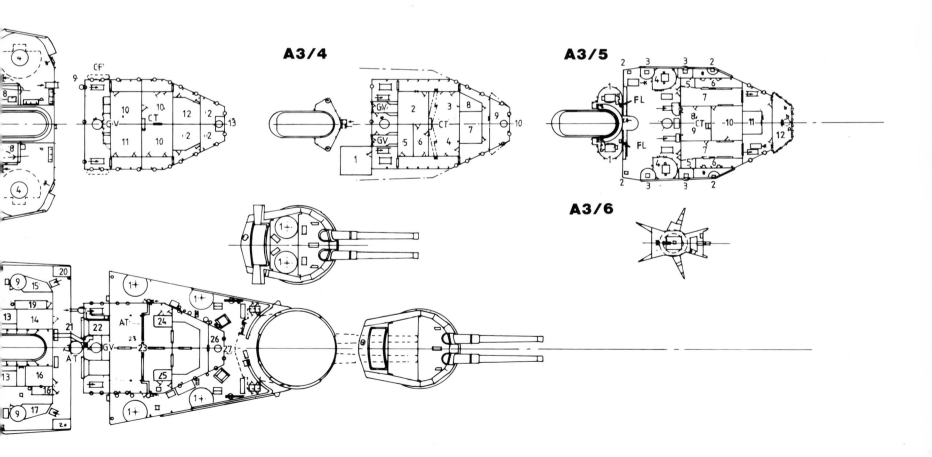

A3/4

A3/5

A3/6

A General arrangements

A4/1

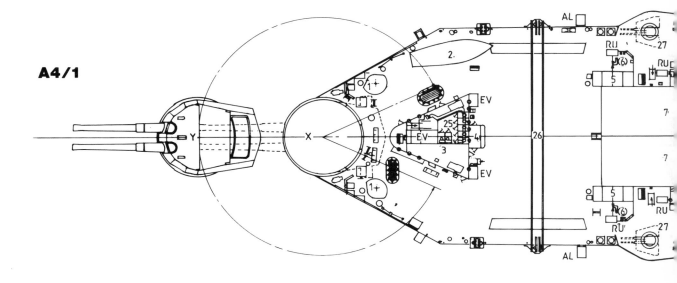

A4/2

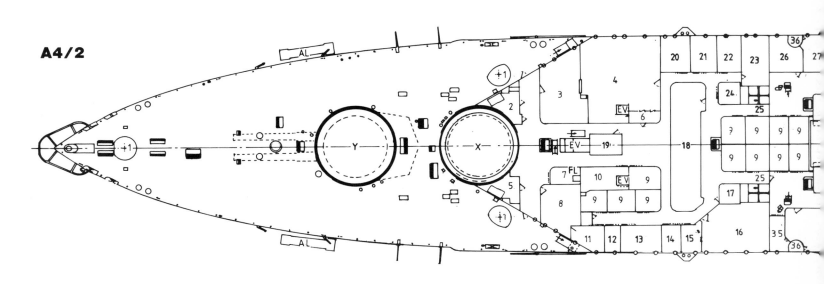

16	Gunroom	33	Warrant officers' galley	50	Gyro adjusting room
17	Marines' office	34	Warrant officers' mess	51	General mess office
18	Catapult mechanism compartment	35	Warrant officers' pantry	52	Regulating training divisional
19	RDF office (Type 282 radar)	36	4in gun support		commander's office
20	Wardroom pantry	37	Funnel uptakes	53	Master-at-arms' cabin
21	Fleet medical officer's cabin	38	Drying room	54	Central store office
22	Fleet marine officer's cabin	39	6in BL gun	55	Ship's office
23	Fleet accountant officer's cabin	40	6in battery voice operator cabinet	56	Chief stokers' and mechanicians'
24	Senior officer's bathroom	41	Dwarf bulkhead		mess
25	Boiler room vent	42	Issue room	57	Chief stokers' and mechanicians'
26	Paymaster commander's cabin	43	Bakery		pantry
27	Engineer commander's cabin	44	Canteen	58	POs' pantry
28	Senior engineer's cabin	45	Ready-use flour store	59	POs' mess
29	Medical officer's cabin	46	Bread cooling room	60	Bookstall
30	Wardroom kitchen	47	6in handing room	61	Darkroom
31	Wardroom galley	48	Communication tube	62	Victualling office
32	Gunroom galley	49	Battery repair compartment	63	Engine room artificers' mess

64	Engine room artificers' pantry
65	Lamp room
66	Bower cable
67	Sheet cable
68	Seamen's heads
69	CPOs' and POs', heads
70	Boys' heads
71	Bow compartment
72	4in HA chain hoist
73	6in shell hoist

AL	Accommodation ladder
AT	Aerial trunk
EV	Exhaust vent
FL	Food lift
A	'A' 15in barbette
B	'B' 15in barbette
X	'X' 15in barbette
Y	'Y' 15in barbette

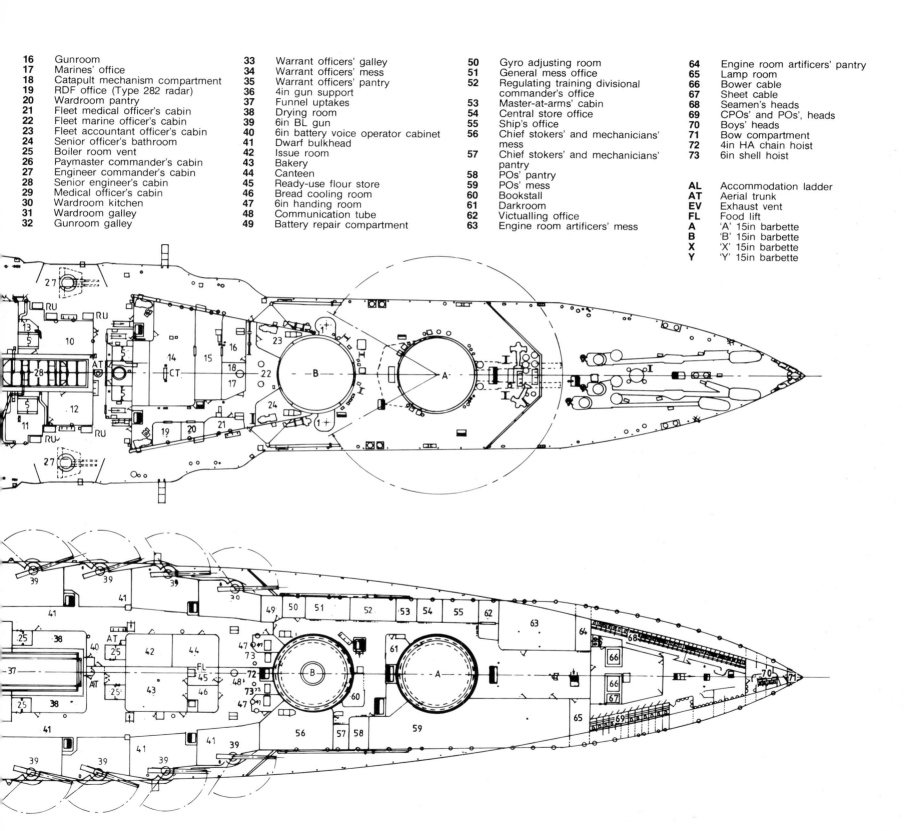

A General arrangements

A4/3 Main deck

1	Sternwalk	**23**	Captain of Fleet's bathroom and WC	**45**	Sergeant of marine's mess	**69**	Cells	
2	Admiral's day cabin	**24**	Store	**46**	PO stokers' mess	**70**	Boatswain's store	
3	Admiral's dining cabin	**25**	Midshipmen's chest	**47**	Boiler room vent	**71**	Petrol working space	
4	Admiral's pantry	**26**	Church	**48**	Stokers' mess	**72**	Paint room	
5	Admiral's secretary's cabin	**27**	Flooding valve space	**49**	Seamen's mess	**73**	Paint store	
6	Fleet engineer officer's cabin	**28**	Torpedo office	**50**	PO stokers' office	**74**	4in HA chain hoist	
7	Officer's cabin	**29**	Engineer's office	**51**	No 1 W/T transmitting room	**75**	6in shell hoist	
8	Admiral's sleeping cabin	**30**	Marines' mess	**52**	Silent cabinet	**76**	Funnel uptakes	
9	Admiral's bathroom	**31**	Central receiving office	**53**	Servery			
10	Admiral's spare cabin	**32**	Central communication office	**54**	Boys' mess	**AT**	Aerial trunk	
11	Flag lieutenant's cabin	**33**	Armament office	**55**	Communication tube	**VE**	Vent and escape	
12	Staff office	**34**	Captain's office	**56**	Regulating petty officer's mess	**EV**	Exhaust vent	
13	Chief of staff's day cabin	**35**	Admiral's galley	**57**	Master-at-arms' mess	**FL**	Food lift	
14	Chief of staff's sleeping cabin	**36**	Admiral's kitchen	**58**	Canteen assistants' mess	**A**	'A' 15in barbette	
15	Chief of staff's bathroom and WC	**37**	H/S receiving office	**59**	Dispensary	**B**	'B' 15in barbette	
16	Printing section office	**38**	H/S transmitting office	**60**	Sickbay	**X**	'X' 15in barbette	
17	Bathroom	**39**	Admiral's cook's cabin	**61**	Operating room	**Y**	'Y' 15in barbette	
18	Duplicating rotaprint office	**40**	Wardroom steward's cabin	**62**	Isolation ward			
19	Captain of Fleet's office	**41**	Admiral's steward's cabin	**63**	CPOs' mess			
20	Captain of Fleet's day cabin	**42**	Admiral's and officers' stewards' and cooks' cabin	**64**	Lime store			
21	Fleet engineer's office	**43**	Cinematograph store	**65**	Sand store			
22	Captain of Fleet's sleeping cabin	**44**	Pantry	**66**	Bower cable			
				67	Sheet cable			
				68	Printing office			

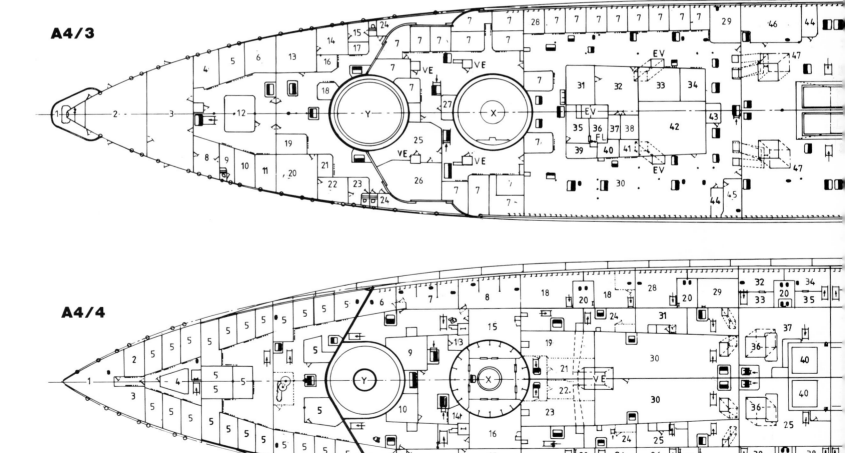

A4/3

A4/4

50

A4/4 Middle deck

1 Writers' main office
2 Officer's second office
3 Officer's main office
4 Outbound correspondence office
5 Officer's cabin
6 Warrant officers' mess stores
7 Gunroom stores
8 Subordinate officers' bathroom
9 Medical distributing station
10 Gun sight gear store
11 Wardroom store
12 Senior officers' bathroom
13 Band instrument room
14 Confidential book room
15 Subordinate officers' dressing room
16 Wardroom stores
17 Commissioned officers' bathroom
18 Marines' store
19 Ordnance artificers' fitting shop
20 Oil fuel working space

21 Ordnance artificers' ready-use store
22 Engineering artificers' ready-use store
23 Engineering artificers' fitting shop
24 Alternator room
25 Marines' hammock and kit-locker room
26 Marines' dressing room
27 Marines' washplace
28 Warrant officers' bathroom
29 Fresh water tank
30 Main machinery and engineer's workshop
31 Officers' bedding store
32 Stoker petty officers' washplace
33 Stoker petty officers' dressing room
34 Leading stokers' washplace
35 Leading stokers' dressing room
36 Vent supply to boiler rooms
37 Stokers' hammock and kit-locker room
38 Seamen's dressing room

39 Seamen's washplace
40 Funnel hatch
41 PO stokers' hammock and kit-locker room
42 Seamen's hammock and kit-locker room
43 Stokers' washplace
44 Stokers' dressing room
45 Searchlight gear store
46 Metadyne store
47 Type 285 radar maintenance gear
48 Engine room artificers' washplace
49 Engine room artificers' dressing room
50 Central store
51 Chief stokers' and mechanicians' washplace
52 Chief stokers' and mechanicians' dressing room
53 POs' dressing room
54 POs' washplace
55 Boys' hammock and kit-locker room
56 Medical distributing station

57 6in shell hoist
58 4in HA chain hoist
59 Communications tube
60 Medical store
61 Flexible hose store
62 Gunnery equipment store
63 Provision room
64 Boys' washplace
65 4in HA calculating position
66 Low power workshop
67 Gunner's store
68 CPOs' dressing room
69 CPOs' washplace
70 Decontamination store
71 Inflammable paint store
72 Clothing store and issue room
73 Shipwright's workshop
74 Shipwright's store
75 Oilstore
76 Anchor gear
77 Canvas and cordage room
78 Lower paint room
79 Water-tight compartment

AT   Aerial trunk
CT   Cable trunk
VE   Vent and escape

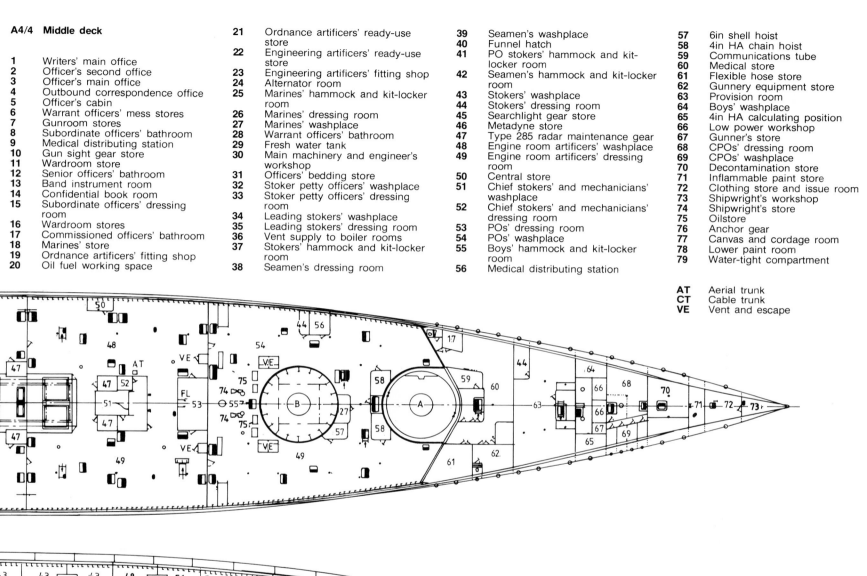

A General arrangements

A4/5 Lower deck

1	Water-tight compartment
2	Admiral's store
3	Captain's store
4	Baggage store
5	Electrical store
6	Electrical and minesweeping store
7	Paymaster's store
8	Awning stowage
9	Air compressor room
10	Hydraulic machinery compartment
11	Hydraulic tank
12	Small arms magazine
13	Revolving hoist to 'Y' barbette
14	Revolving hoist to 'X' barbette
15	Dynamo room
16	Gyro compass room
17	Centre gear room
18	Evaporator room
19	Rum store
20	Oil fuel tank
21	Wing gear room
22	Wing turbine room
23	Centre turbine room
24	Boiler room

25	Cable passage
26	Searchlight stabiliser room
27	Central store
28	Engineer's spare gear store
29	Lower steering position
30	Protected navigational plotting office
31	Switchboard room
32	6in shell hoist
33	4in HA chain hoist
34	Revolving hoist to 'B' barbette
35	Torpedo gunner's store
36	Provision room
37	15in transmitting station
38	Secondary armament clock rooms
39	Gunsight gear store
40	Revolving hoist to 'A' barbette
41	Flour store
42	Paravane store
43	Spare armature room

44	Fresh water tank
45	Chart and chronometer room
46	Cable locker

DB Double bottom compartment

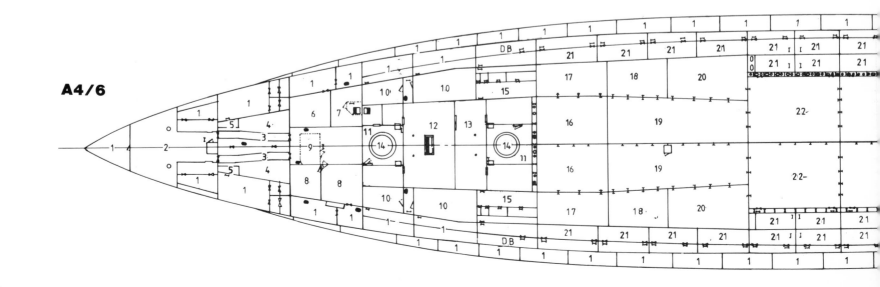

A4/5

A4/6

52

A4/6 Platform deck

1 Water-tight compartment
2 Steering gear compartment
3 Cable passage
4 Fresh water tank
5 Palm compartment
6 Electrical store
7 Electrical and minesweeping store
8 Paymaster's store
9 Awning stowage
10 4in HA magazine
11 15in handing room
12 'Y' magazine
13 'X' magazine
14 Revolving hoist
15 Shaft passage
16 Centre gear room

17 Evaporator room
18 Wing gear room
19 Centre turbine room
20 Wing turbine room
21 Oil fuel tank
22 Boiler room
23 Dynamo room
24 Silent compartment
25 Air space
26 Sub-calibre and small arms magazine
27 High angle control position
28 Telephone exchange
29 Upper pom-pom magazine
30 'B' magazine
31 'A' magazine
32 Provision room
33 Gunner's store

34 Cool room
35 Cordage store
36 Cold room
37 Refrigerating machinery compartment
38 Capstan engine room
39 Petrol tank
40 4in HA chain hoist
41 6in shell hoist
42 No 2 W/T transmitter room

DB Double bottom compartment

A4/7 Lower platform

1 Air space
2 Engineer's spare gear store
3 Bomb room
4 6in magazine
5 6in shell hoists

A4/7

A General arrangements

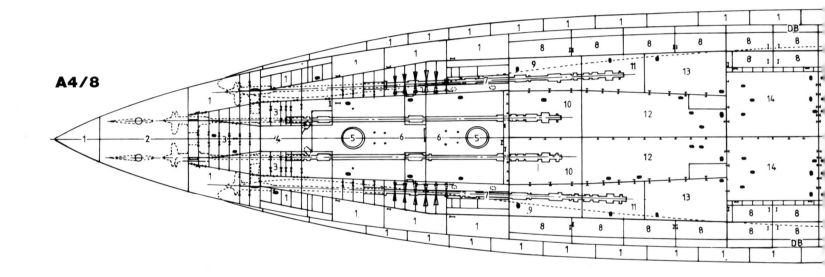

A4/8

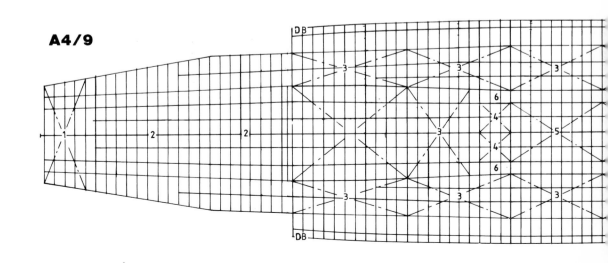

A4/9

A4/9 Double bottom

1 Fresh water tank
2 Water-tight compartment
3 Oil fuel compartment
4 Overflow feed tank
5 Feed tank
6 Reserve feed tank
7 Air space

DB Double bottom compartment

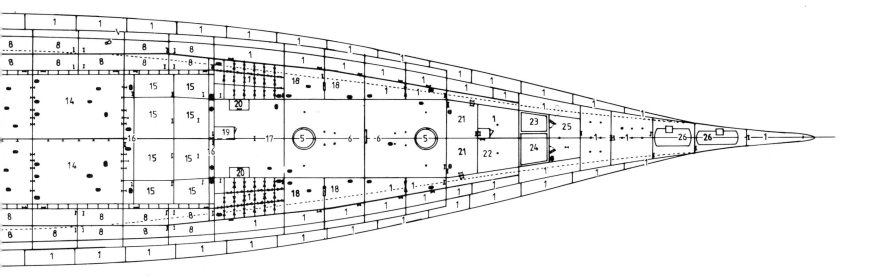

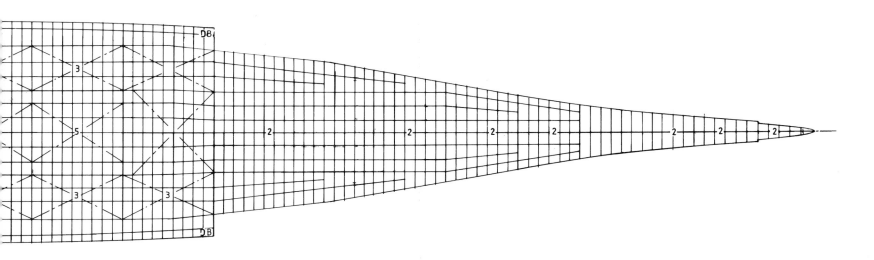

A General arrangements

A5   EXTERNAL PROFILE 1943

A5

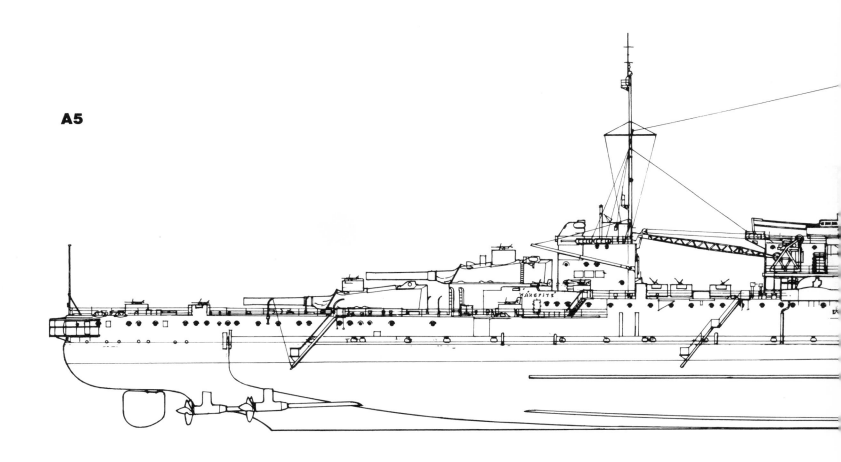

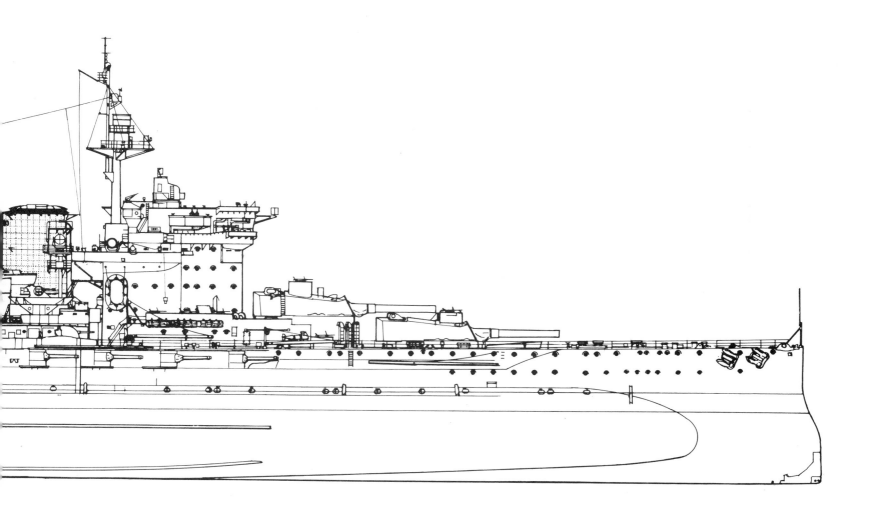

B Hull construction

B1   **EXPANSION OF OUTER BOTTOM PLATING (1/400 scale)**

1	20lb* plate
2	25lb plate
3	30lb plate
4	35lb plate
5	40lb plate
6	Armour
7	Line of bulge plating
8	Longitudinals
9	Main discharge
10	Main inlet
11	Recess for shaft
12	Shaft brackets
13	30lb doubling
14	35lb doubling
15	Oil-tight bulkhead
16	Water-tight bulkhead

*1 square foot of ordinary mild steel plate 1in thick weighs 40.8lb. Thus a plate with 'thickness' shown as 20lb is approximately ½in thick.

a	Forecastle deck
b	Upper deck
c	Main deck
d	Middle deck
e	Lower deck

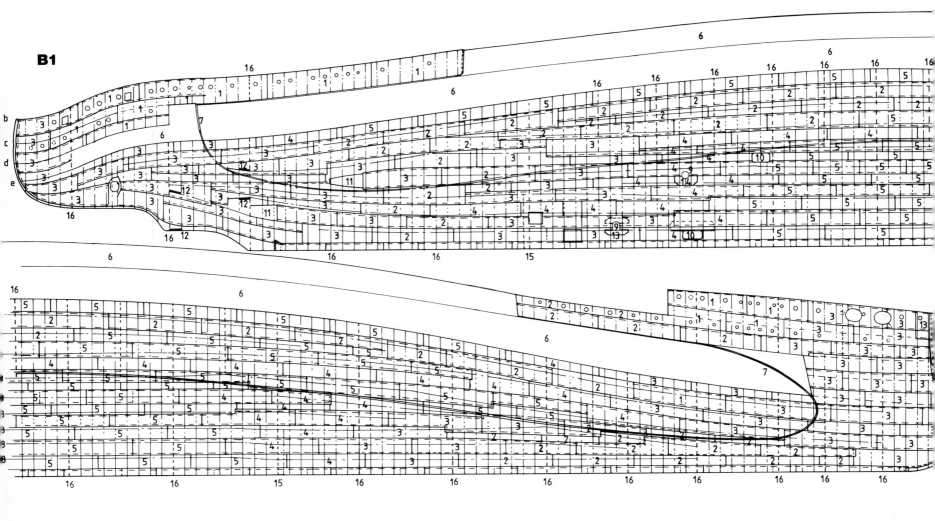

B2 EXPANSION OF BULGE PLATING
(1/800 scale)

1 Fender
2 Bilge keel

B2

153·5   32·75

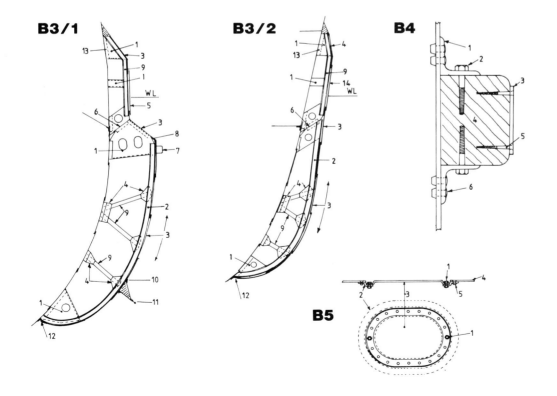

B3/1   **B3/2**   **B4**

WL   WL

B5

B3 **TYPICAL SECTIONS OF BULGE**
(1/200 scale)

B3/1 Section at 153.5 station

B3/2 Section at 32.75 station

1 20lb flange bracket
2 9in × 3.5in × 3.5in channel bar
3 22.5lb plate
4 20lb plate
5 30lb plate
6 30lb crown plate
7 Fender
8 6in × 6in angle bar
9 6in × 3in × 3in channel bar
10 4.5in × 4.5in angle bar
11 10lb bulb plate
12 30lb flanged plate
13 3.5in × 3.5in angle bar
14 25lb plate

B4 **BULGE FENDER (no scale)**

1 5in × 5in × 0.5in angle bar
2 Coach screw
3 Mild steel plate
4 Wood
5 5in galvanised screw
6 Rivets

B5 **BULGE MANHOLE COVER (no scale)**

1 ¾in bolt
2 Stamped steel ring
3 Stamped steel cover
4 Bulge plating
5 Rivet

B Hull construction

B6 **MIDSHIP SECTION (after 1937; no scale)**

1 Vertical keel and centre-line bulkhead
2 Double bottom bracket-type frame
3 Inner bottom plating
4 Boiler room
5 Boiler uptake
6 Longitudinal bulkhead
7 Cable passage
8 Oil fuel tank
9 Double bottom compartment
10 Bulge
11 Longitudinal girder
12 Deep beam
13 Armour grating
14 Deck beams
15 Side armour
16 Air space

A Forecastle deck
B Upper deck
C Main deck
D Middle deck

B7 **TYPES OF LONGITUDINALS AND FRAMES WITH DOUBLE BOTTOM (no scale)**

1 Lightening hole
2 Lap joint
3 Angle connection to bracket frame
4 Angle bar
5 Drain hole
6 Angle connection to oil-tight frame
8 Water-tight liner
9 Stiffeners

A Non water-tight longitudinal
B Vertical keel within double bottom
C Lightened plate frames
D Water-tight frame
E Bracket frame

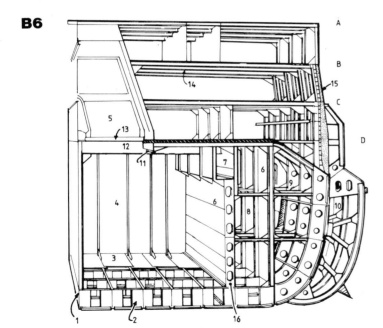

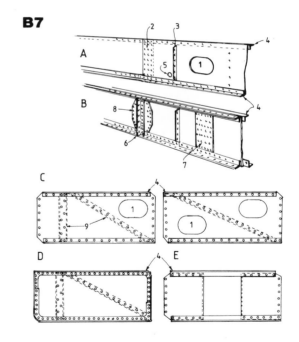

B8   LINES (1937 onwards)

B8/1 Body plan (1/225 scale)

B8/2 Profile (1/900 scale)

1 Bulge
2 Bilge keel
3 Bulge fender
4 160lb armour
5 240lb armour
6 520lb armour

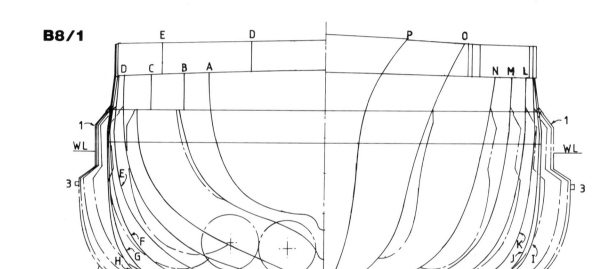

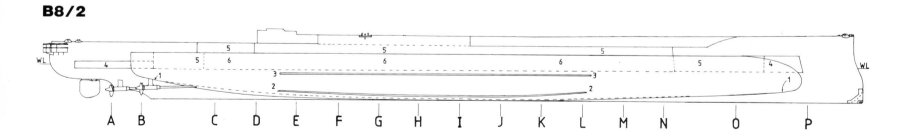

B Hull construction

B9   ARMOUR AND PROTECTIVE PLATING (after 1937; 1/900 scale)

B9/1   Transverse sections (see B9/2)

B9/2   Profile

B9/3   Roof of Captain's shelter

B9/4   Plan of upper bridge and compass platform

B9/5   Plan of Admiral's bridge

B9/6   Plan of upper conning tower

B9/7   Forecastle deck

B9/8   Upper deck

B9/9   Main deck

B9/10   Middle deck

B9/11   Lower deck

B9/12   Hold

1	15lb
2	20lb
3	25lb
4	40lb
5	50lb
6	60lb
7	70lb
8	80lb
9	100lb
10	120lb
11	160lb
12	240lb
13	280lb
14	360lb
15	400lb
16	520lb
17	Communications tube

A   D1 (HT – high-tensile)
B   NMBP (nickel and manganese bullet proof)

C   NC (non-cemented)
D   DQ
E   HT (high-tensile)
F   DI
R   Reducing down to
X   Doubling
CT   Cable trunk
SH   Shell hoist

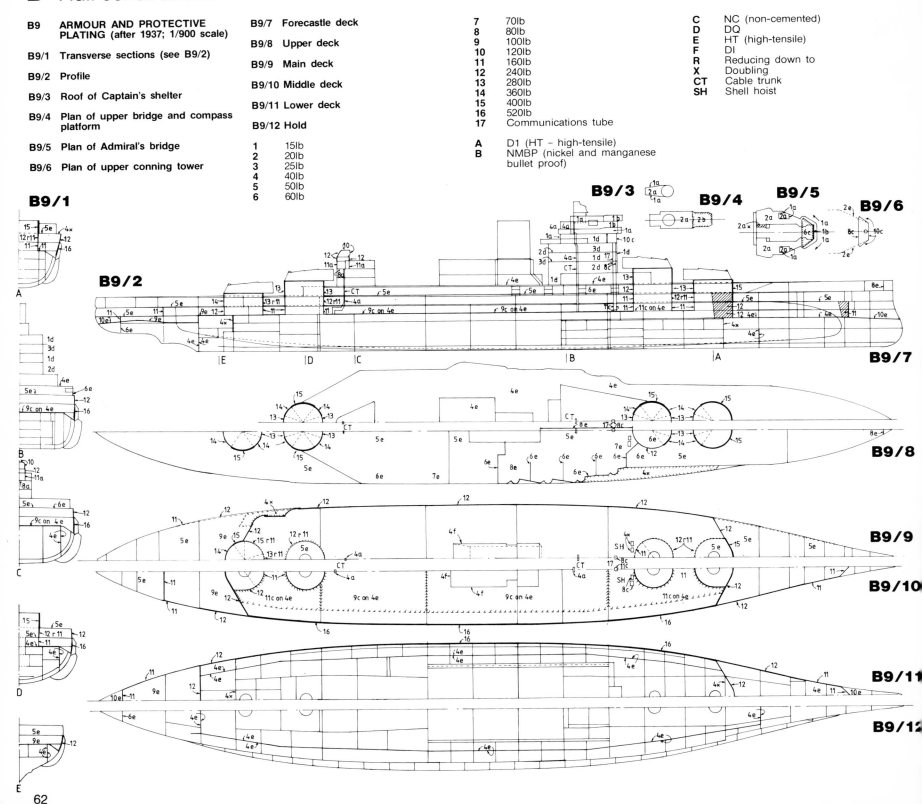

B10 SECTION OF SIDE ARMOUR AMIDSHIPS (no scale)

1 240lb armour
2 520lb armour
3 3in teak backing
4 Backing plate
5 'Z' bar frames
6 Intercostal stiffener
7 Main deck
8 Middle deck
9 Longitudinal protective bulkhead
10 Double bottom lightened plate frame
11 Armour shelf
12 Cover plate
13 Channel frame

B11 BOW STRUCTURE (1/100 scale)

1 Stern casting
2 Deck support lugs
3 Enlarged section of stem casting
4 Rabbet for side plate
5 Paravane foot
6 Vertical keel
7 Contour plate
8 Floor plates
9 Angle bulb deck beams
10 Channel bar deck beams

A Forecastle deck
B Upper deck
C Main deck
D Middle deck
E Lower deck
F Platform deck

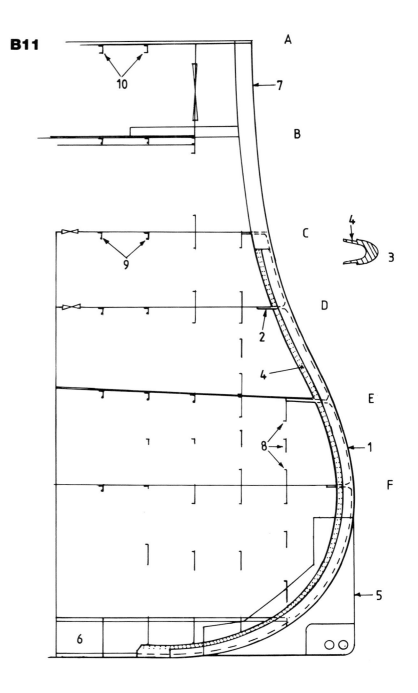

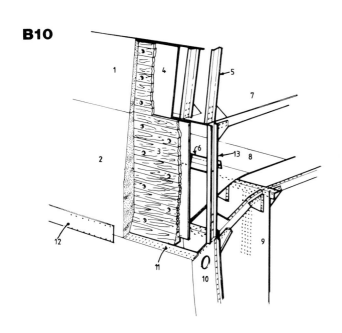

B Hull construction

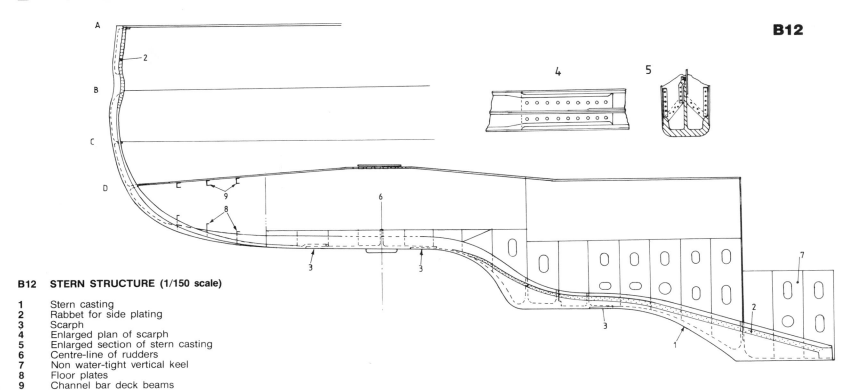

B12

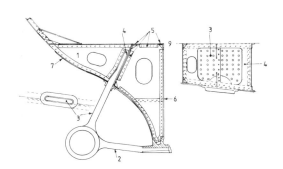

B13/1

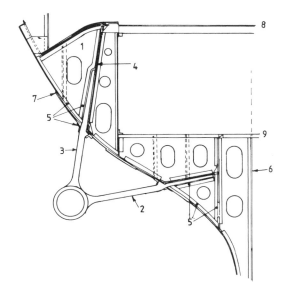

B13/2

B12 STERN STRUCTURE (1/150 scale)

1	Stern casting
2	Rabbet for side plating
3	Scarph
4	Enlarged plan of scarph
5	Enlarged section of stern casting
6	Centre-line of rudders
7	Non water-tight vertical keel
8	Floor plates
9	Channel bar deck beams

A	Upper deck
B	Main deck
C	Middle deck
D	Lower deck

B13 STRUCTURE IN WAY OF SHAFT BRACKETS (1/100 scale)

B13/1 Starboard inner shaft 'A' bracket

B13/2 Starboard outer shaft 'B' bracket

1	Lightened floor plate
2	Lower palm
3	Upper palm
4	Palm plate
5	Angle bars
6	Non water-tight vertical keel
7	Side plating
8	Lower deck
9	Platform deck

C Machinery

C1 GENERAL ARRANGEMENTS OF ENGINE ROOMS 1915 (scale 1/200)

C1/1 Plan of engine rooms

C1/2 Longitudinal section of centre engine room

1 Low pressure ahead and astern turbine
2 High pressure ahead turbine
3 High pressure astern turbine
4 Main condenser
5 Air pump
6 Evaporator
7 Distiller
8 Main circulating pump
9 Auxiliary condenser
10 Auxiliary air pump
11 Electric lift
12 Feed tank
13 Feed water heater
14 Telephone cabinet
15 Steering engines
16 Distiller pump
17 Oil fuel tank pump
18 Oil cooler
19 Water service pump
20 Fire and bilge pump
21 Main bearing feed lubrication pumps
22 Plummer block feed lubrication pumps
23 Fresh water pump
24 Oil drain tank
25 Auxiliary circulating pump
26 Oil fuel pump
27 Shaft
28 Platform
29 Oil settling tank

LW Ladderway (over)
NV Natural vent
VE Vent exhaust
VS Vent supply

C1/1

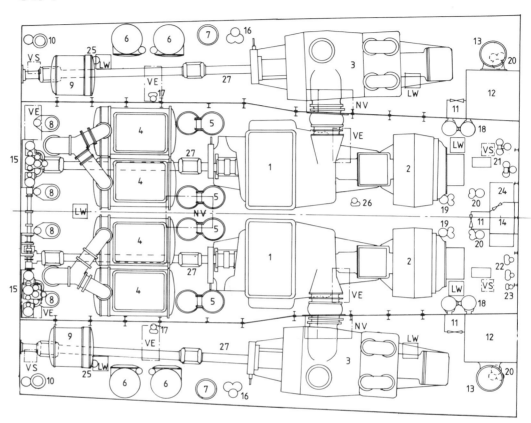

C1/2

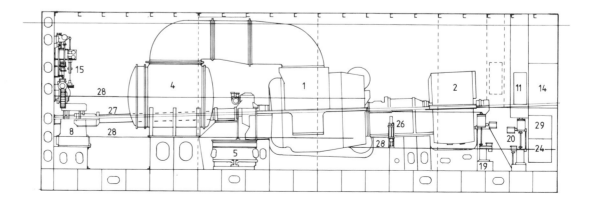

C Machinery

C2/1

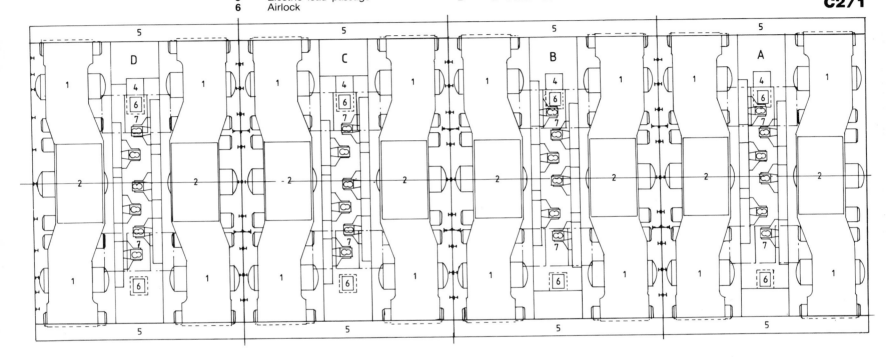

C2/2

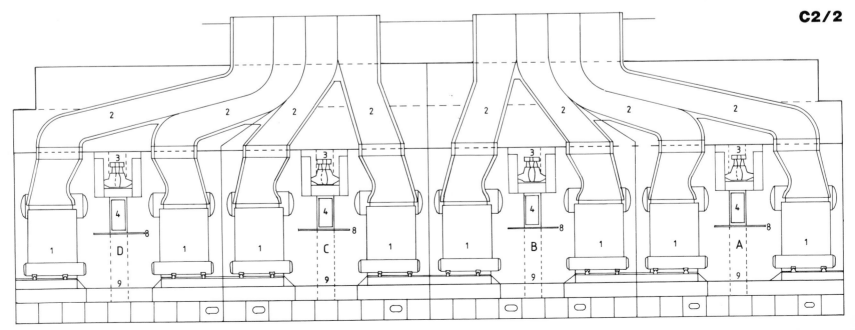

C3 GENERAL ARRANGEMENTS OF ENGINE ROOMS 1937 (1/200 scale)

C3/1 Plan of engine rooms

C3/2 Longitudinal section of centre turbine and gear room

1 Low pressure ahead and astern turbine
2 High pressure ahead turbine
3 Gear case
4 Condenser
5 Thrust block
6 Torsion meter
7 Turbo-driven fire and bilge pump
8 Fire and bilge pump
9 Motor-driven forced lubricating pump
10 Turbo-driven forced lubricating pump
11 Motor-driven air compressor
12 Air receiver
13 Forced lubricating discharge filter
14 Forced lubricating oil cooler
15 Calorifier
16 Auxiliary condenser
17 Auxiliary air pump
18 Evaporator
19 Ejector condenser
20 Main circulating pump
21 Motor-driven extraction pump
22 Turbo-driven extraction pump
23 Harbour service feed pump
24 Feed heater
25 Main feed pump
26 Turbo cruising feed pump
27 Closed feed air ejectors
28 Closed feed control valve
29 Feed tank to wing turbine room
30 Feed tank to centre turbine room
31 Oil fuel transfer pump
32 Plummer block
33 Auxiliary circulating pump
34 Motor-driven fire and bilge pump
35 Telephone cabinet
36 Variable delivery pump
37 Supply fan
38 Exhaust fan
39 Platform
40 Floor
41 Feed heater drain pump
42 Feed supply pump
43 Oil fuel tank
44 Main inlet
45 Main discharge

LW Ladderway

A Evaporator room
B Centre gear room
C Wing gear room
D Wing turbine room
E Centre turbine room

C3/1

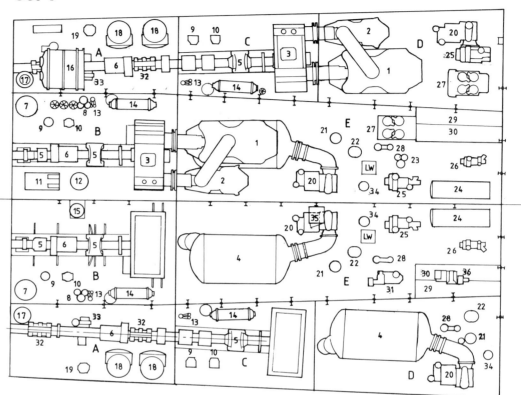

C3/2

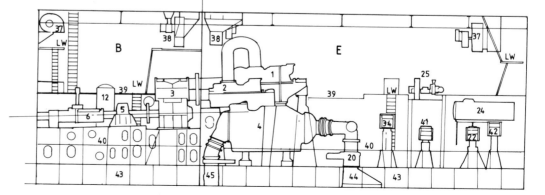

C Machinery

1   No 1 boiler room
2   No 2 boiler room
3   No 3 boiler room
4   No 4 boiler room
5   No 5 boiler room
6   No 6 boiler room
7   Turbo forced-draught fan
8   Auxiliary boiler
9   Oil fuel heaters
10   Oil fuel filters
11   Emergency bilge pump
12   Auxiliary feed pump
13   Grease extractors
14   Fire and bilge pump
15   Reserve feed tanks
16   Platform

AL   Airlock
AS   Airspace
BU   Boiler uptake
CP   Cable passage
LW   Ladderway
VS   Ventilation supply

C4/1

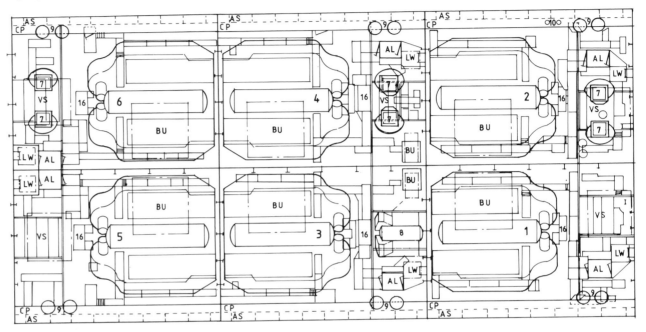

C4/2

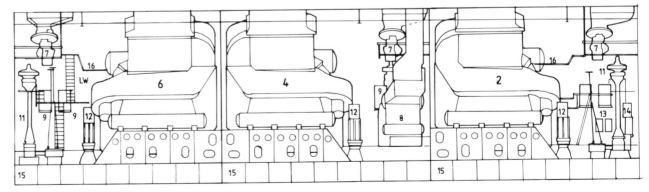

C5 GENERAL ARRANGEMENTS OF STEERING GEAR COMPARTMENT 1915 (1/200 scale)

C5/1 Plan

C5/2 Longitudinal section

1 Water-tight armoured bulkhead
2 Rudder casting
3 Screw gear
4 Tiller compartment
5 Palm compartment
6 Steering compartment
7 Auxiliary motor
8 Steering cabinet
9 Escape (over)
10 Gear wheels
11 Rudder
12 Inner shaft bracket
13 Armoured lower deck

LW Ladder way

C6 ARRANGEMENTS OF PROPELLER SHAFTS 1915 (1/300 scale)

C6/1 Plan

C6/2 Longitudinal section

1 Inner shaft bracket
2 Outer shaft bracket
3 Plummer blocks
4 Shaft coupling
5 Bridge over shaft
6 Thrust block

C5/1

C5/2

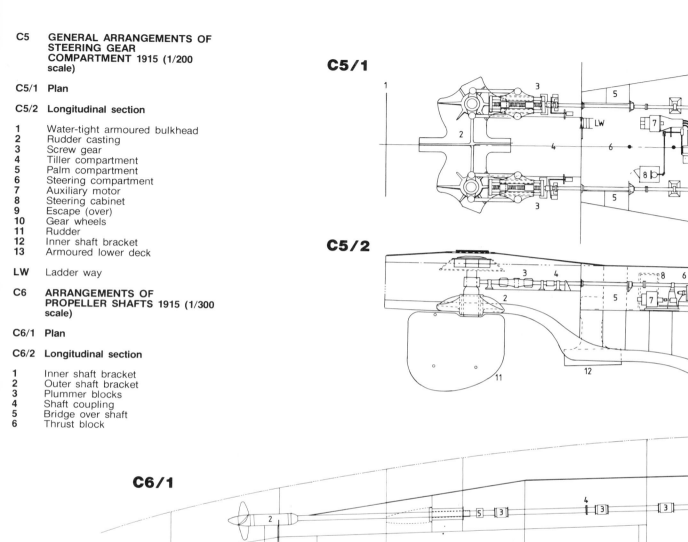

C6/1

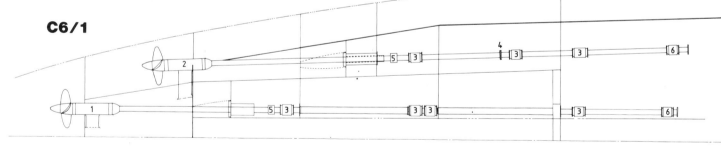

C6/2

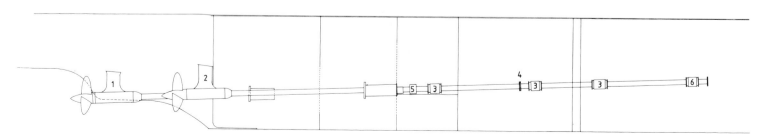

C Machinery

C6/3

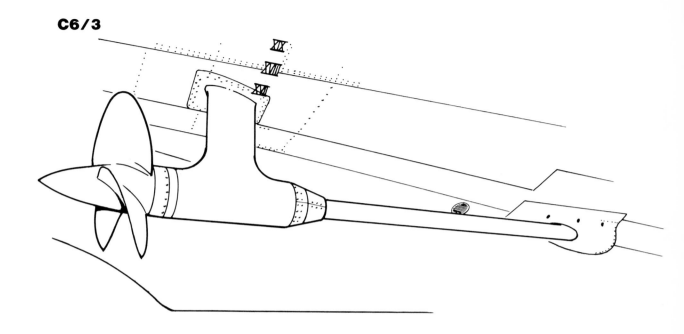

C7/1

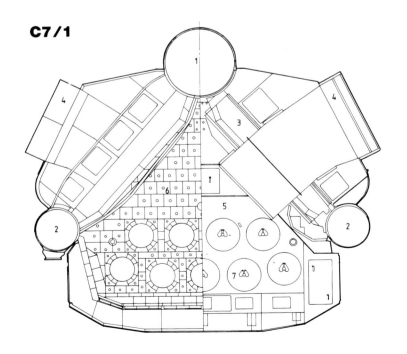

C7/2

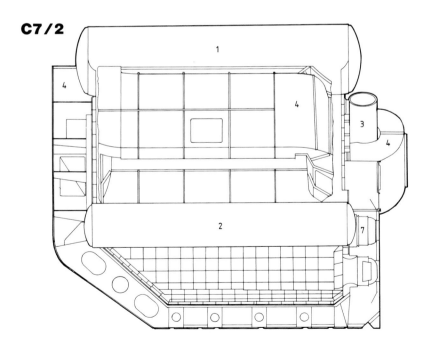

D Accommodation

D1   **SENIOR OFFICERS' ACCOMMODATION 1915 (main deck aft; 1/200 scale)**

1   Admiral's day cabin
2   Admiral's dining cabin
3   Admiral's sleeping cabin
4   Admiral's bathroom and WC
5   Admiral's spare cabin
6   Admiral's pantry
7   Secretary's cabin
8   Flag commander's cabin
9   Flag lieutenant's cabin
10   Admiral's lobby
11   Bookcase
12   Card table
13   Roll top desk
14   Stove
15   Cupboard
16   Kneehole table
17   Sideboard
18   Dining table
19   Hinged table
20   Shelf (over)
21   Bedstead (drawers under)
22   Wardrobe
23   Drawers
24   Dressing table
25   Tank (over)
26   Bath
27   Wash basin
28   Rack (over)
29   Tin bath (over)
30   Hand-through
31   Electric food heater
32   Sink
33   Lockers
34   Working top
35   Berth (trays under)
36   Escape from steering gear compartment
37   Curtain
38   Water-tight compartment

EF   Exhaust fan
ER   Electric radiator
LW   Ladderway
SF   Supply fan
WH   Water-tight hatch

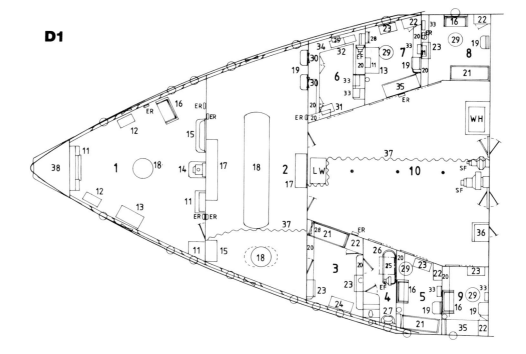

D1

D Accommodation

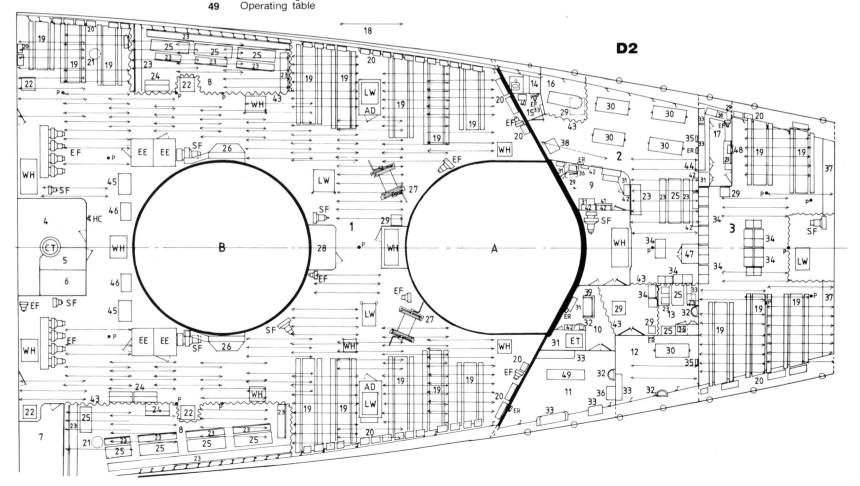

D2 **ACCOMMODATION ON**
MAIN DECK 1915 (1/200 scale)

1   Junior rates' mess
2   Sickbay
3   Petty officers' mess
4   Flour store
5   Auxiliary wireless telegraph office
6   Silent cabinet
7   Biscuit store
8   Reading room
9   Dispensary
10 Surgeon's examining room
11 Operating room
12 Isolation ward
13 Sick berth staff's mess
14 WC
15 Annexe
16 Bathroom
17 Petty officers' pantry
18 Hammock billet
19 Mess table
20 Mess rack and ditty box
21 Scuttle to coal bunker
22 Water-tight hatch to coal bunker

23 Seat
24 Ship's library
25 Table
26 Heater
27 Cordage reel
28 Flooding valves compartment
29 Fresh water tank (over)
30 Swinging cot (2-tier)
31 Cupboard
32 Wash basin
33 Shelves
34 Lockers
35 Cot ladder
36 Sink
37 Hammock stowage
38 Refrigerator
39 Kneehole table
40 Venereal trough
41 Poison cupboard
42 Rack (over)
43 Curtain
44 Operating table (stowed)
45 6in ammunition hoist
46 6in dredger hoist
47 Bedding cupboard
48 Hand-through
49 Operating table

A   'A' barbette
B   'B' barbette
P   Pillar
AD Air-tight door trunk
CT Communications tube
EE Escape and exhaust trunk
EF Exhaust fan
ER Electric radiator
ET Escape trunk
HC Hose connection
LW Ladderway
SF Supply fan
WH Water-tight hatch

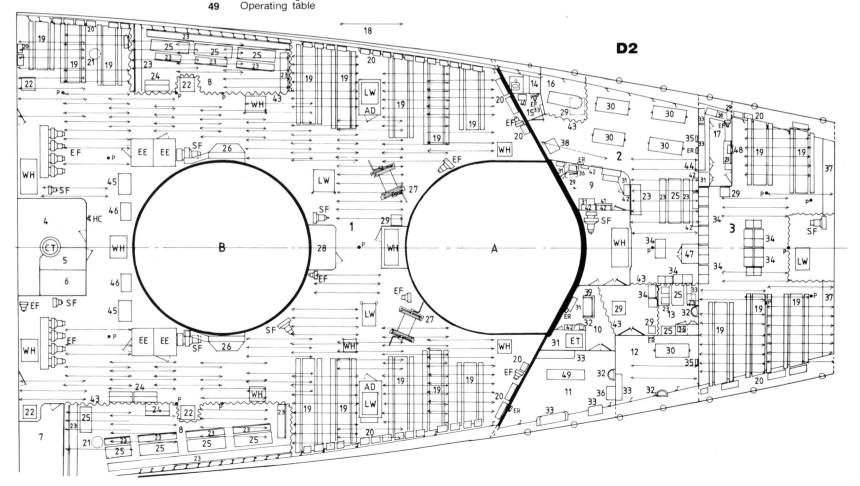

D3 TYPICAL WASHPLACE, HAMMOCK AND LOCKER ROOM 1915 (1/200 scale)

1 Stoker petty officers' washplace
2 Seamen's washplace
3 Seamen's hammock and locker room
4 Oil fuel working space
5 Ventilator to boiler room
6 Hammock stowage
7 Wash basins
8 Lockers (3-tier)
9 Drain tank
10 Water tank
11 Gutterway
12 Seat
13 Tin bath (over)
14 Kit-lockers (3-tier)
15 Escape from electric leads passage
16 Lift motor
17 Electric lift

D4 WC ARRANGEMENT

1 Dished doors
2 Panelling
3 Salt water main
4 Pushcock
5 Backrest
6 Vent pipe
7 Rubber
8 Metal tubing
9 Step
10 Soil pipe
11 Tiled floor on cement

D3

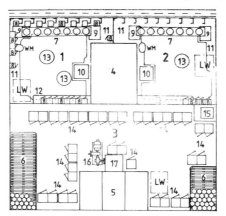

D4

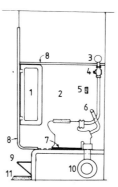

E Superstructure

E1 AFTER SUPERSTRUCTURE 1915
(1/200 scale)

E1/1 Signalling searchlight platform
(fitted in 1917)

E1/2 Plan of after shelter deck

E1/3 Profile of after shelter deck

E1/4 General view of after shelter deck
1920 (no scale)

1   Stern light
2   Mainmast
3   Torpedo director tower
4   40in searchlight
5   Aerial screen
6   Derrick stanchion
7   Sanitary tank
8   Fresh water tank
9   Forge
10 Funnel of admiral's galley
11 Work bench
12 Ensign staff (war position)
13 40ft derrick
14 Mainmast stays
15 Searchlight control position

D   Davit
E   Eyeplate
H   Hatch
L   Ladder
MH Manhole
MV Mushroom vent
S   Scupper
SL Skylight
SV Swan-neck valve
VE Vent exhaust

E1/1

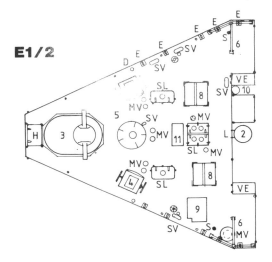

E1/2

E1/4

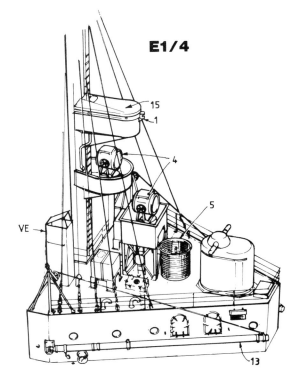

E1/3

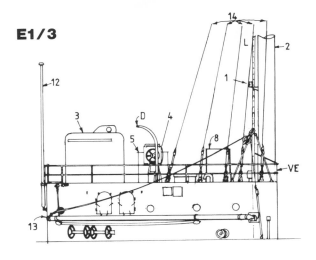

E2   AFTER FUNNEL PLATFORMS 1915
(1/200 scale)

E2/1   Searchlight platform

E2/2   Searchlight control platform

E2/3   Plan of after funnel

E2/4   Profile of after funnel

1   Evershed transmitter
2   Searchlight controller
3   40in searchlight
4   Exhaust pipe opening

D   Davit
EP   Exhaust pipe
H   Hatch
L   Ladder
MV   Mushroom vent

E2/1

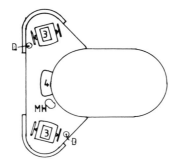

E2/2

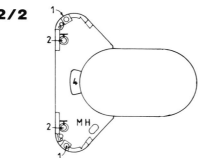

E2/4

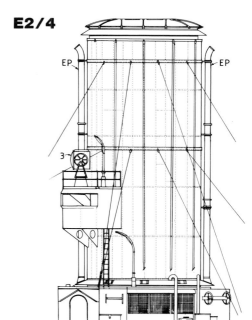

E2/3

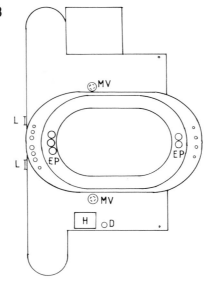

E Superstructure

E3 **FORWARD FUNNEL AND SUPERSTRUCTURE 1915 (1/200 scale)**

E3/1 **Plan of shelter deck**

1   Foremast strut
2   Sanitary tank
3   Arched opening
4   Foremast
5   Vent to boiler room
6   Navigating officer's cabin
7   Signal house
8   Officers' WC
9   Blast screen
10 Signal officer's cabin
11 Officers' oilskin store
12 Signal distributing office
13 'B' barbette
14 3pdr gun
15 Maxim gun
16 Communication tube
17 Fresh water tank
18 Admiral's sea cabin
19 Admiral's charthouse
20 Flag-locker
21 Sounding machine
22 Forward night gun control
23 Searchlight controller
24 Evershed transmitter
25 Conning tower
26 Vicker's range clock
27 15in control tower
28 Revolution telegraph
29 Engine telegraph
30 Steering wheel
31 Navigation light
32 40in searchlight
33 Evershed indicator
34 Station crew's shelter
35 Charthouse
36 Captain's sea cabin
37 Bolted plate (for lowering topmast)
38 6in gun direction tower
39 Weatherproof shelter
40 Gyro compass
41 Compass
42 Semaphore

AS	Awning stanchion	**MH**	Manhole
AT	Aerial trunk	**MV**	Mushroom vent
D	Davit	**R**	Reel
EP	Exhaust pipe	**S**	Scupper
H	Hatch	**SL**	Skylight
HC	Hose connection	**SV**	Swan-neck valve
L	Ladder	**WL**	Wash deck locker
LV	Light and vent		

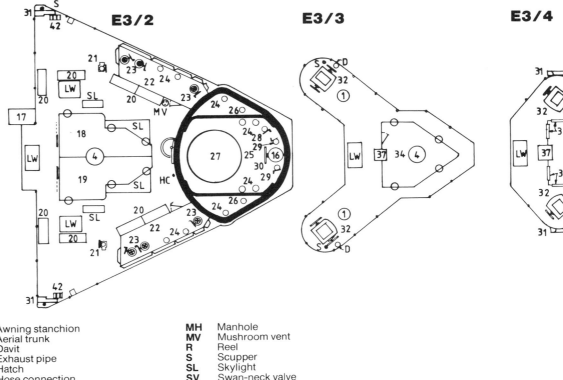

E3/2   E3/3   E3/4

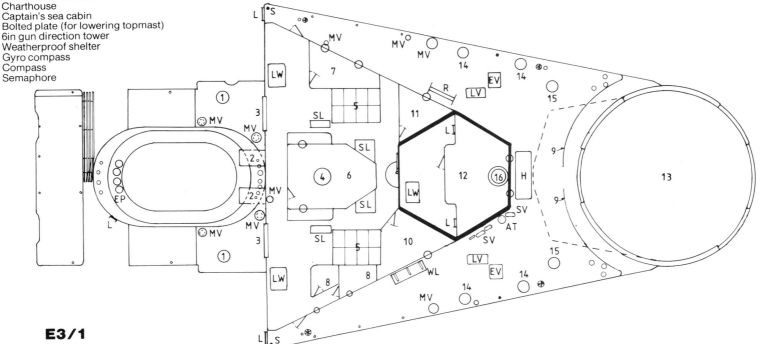

E3/1

E3/5

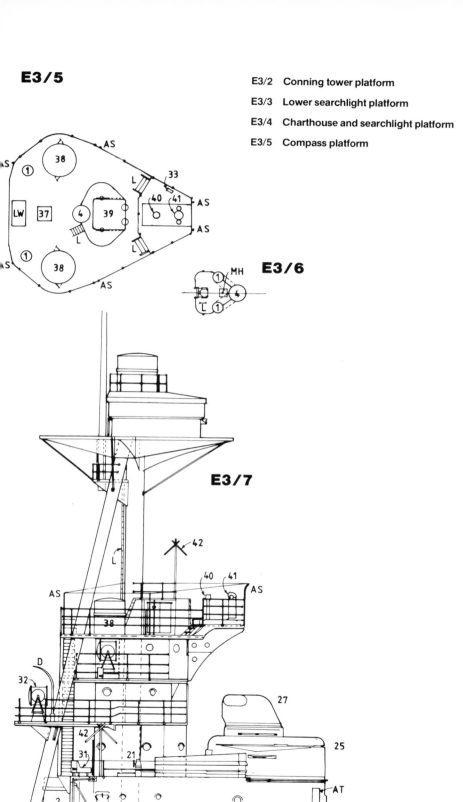

E3/2   Conning tower platform

E3/3   Lower searchlight platform

E3/4   Charthouse and searchlight platform

E3/5   Compass platform

E3/6   Lower platform

E3/7   Profile of forward superstructure

E3/8   General view (no scale)

E3/6

E3/7

E3/8

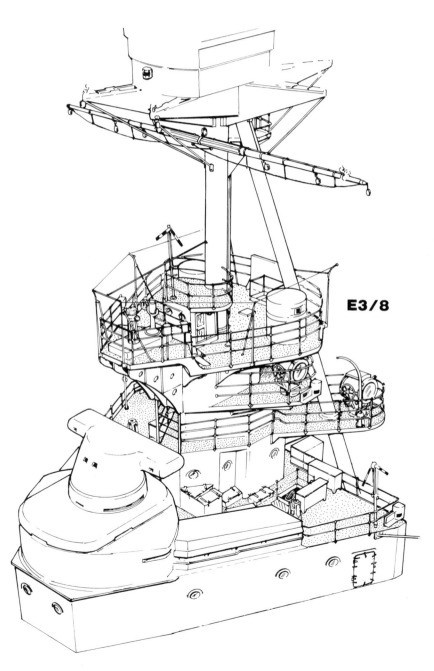

E Superstructure

E4 **FORECASTLE DECK 1915 (1/200 scale)**

1 27ft whaler
2 16ft dinghy
3 32ft galley
4 40ft derrick
5 Boat hoist derrick
6 Rack for 6in shell
7 45ft admiral's barge
8 50ft pinnace
9 42ft launch
10 36ft pinnace

11 Shutter
12 Lifebelt locker
13 Quartermaster's locker
14 Seaboat gear locker
15 3in ready-use ammunition locker
16 6in BL gun
17 3in HA gun
18 Sighting hood
19 Scuttle
20 34ft derrick
21 Lead men's platform
22 32ft cutter

AS Awning stanchion
B Bollard
D Davit
EW Electric winch
F Fairlead
H Hatch
HC Hose connection
L Ladder
LV Light and vent
MV Mushroom vent

OF Oil-fuel filling
R Reel
S Scupper
SL Skylight
SV Swan-neck valve
V Vent
VE Vent exhaust
VS Vent supply
WL Wash deck locker

E4

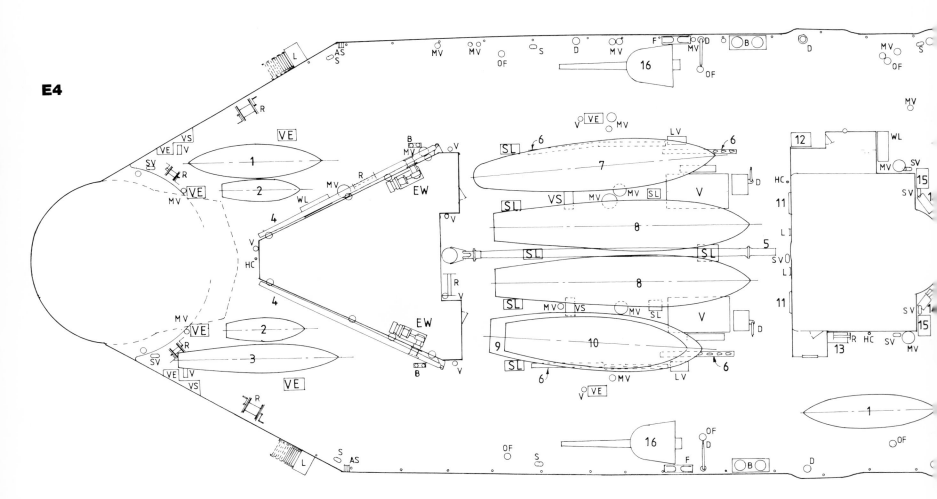

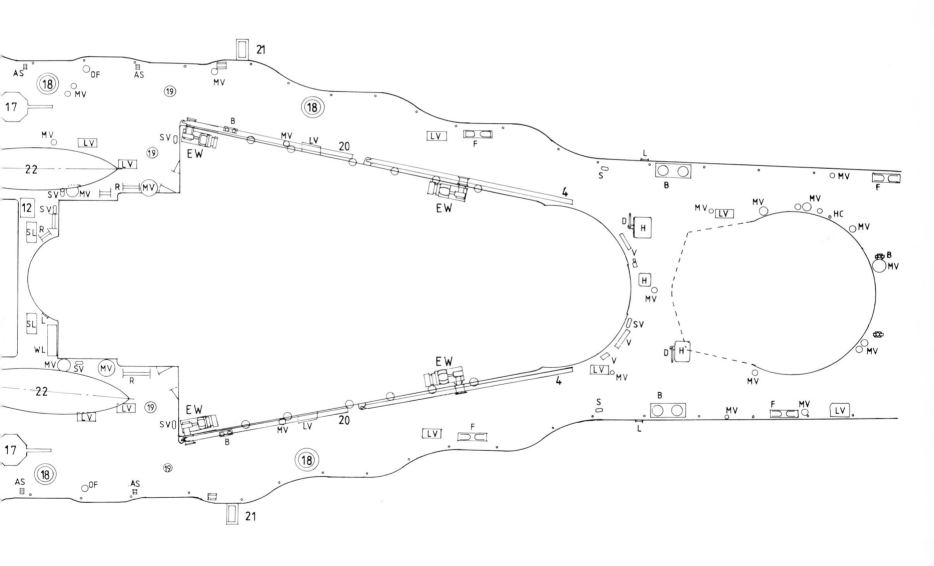

E Superstructure

E5/1

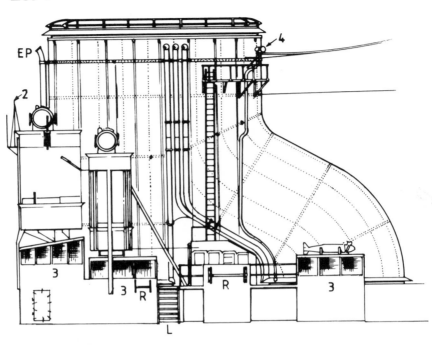

E5/2

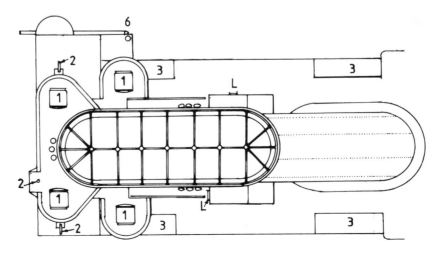

E5/3

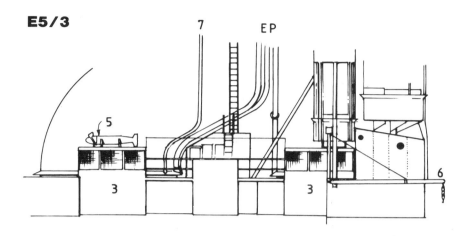

E5/4

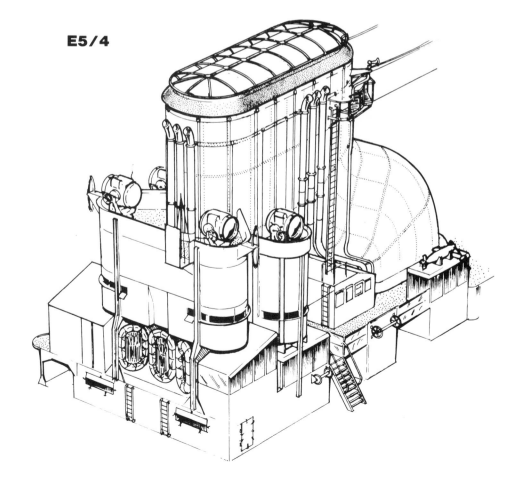

E Superstructure

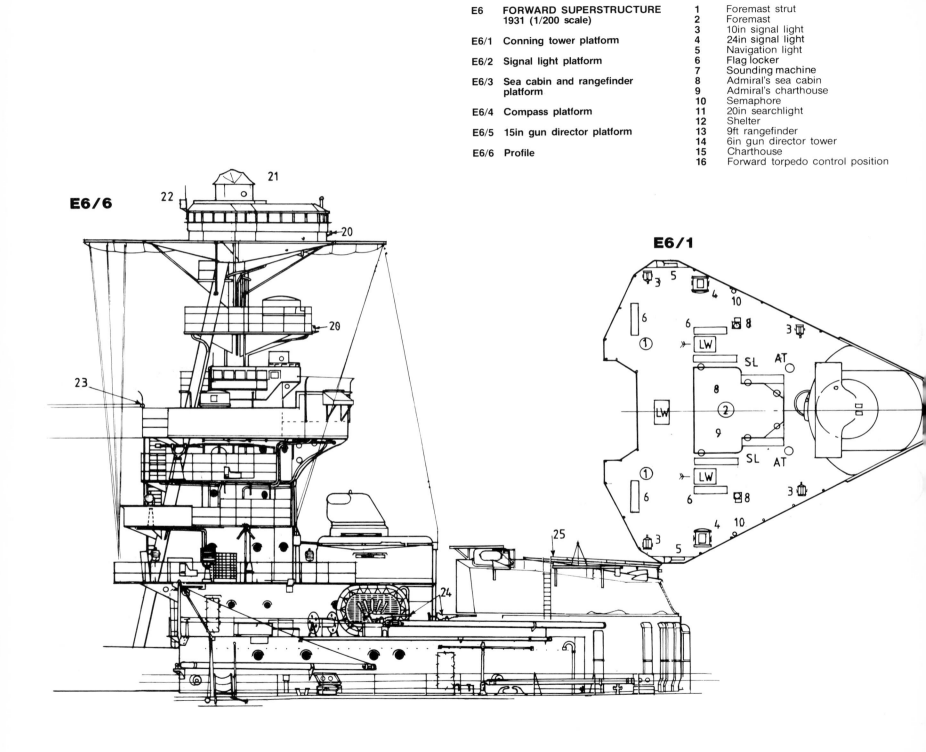

E6	FORWARD SUPERSTRUCTURE 1931 (1/200 scale)
E6/1	Conning tower platform
E6/2	Signal light platform
E6/3	Sea cabin and rangefinder platform
E6/4	Compass platform
E6/5	15in gun director platform
E6/6	Profile

1	Foremast strut
2	Foremast
3	10in signal light
4	24in signal light
5	Navigation light
6	Flag locker
7	Sounding machine
8	Admiral's sea cabin
9	Admiral's charthouse
10	Semaphore
11	20in searchlight
12	Shelter
13	9ft rangefinder
14	6in gun director tower
15	Charthouse
16	Forward torpedo control position

17	Compass
18	Gyro compass
19	15in gun director tower
20	Steaming light
21	High-Angle Control System Mk I
22	Type 75 short range W/T unit
23	Siren control pulley
24	3pdr saluting gun
25	Flying-off platform

AS	Awning stanchion
AT	Aerial trunk
L	Ladder
LW	Ladderway
SL	Skylight

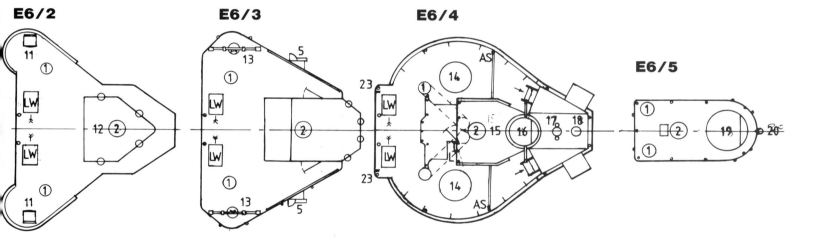

E6/2   **E6/3**   **E6/4**   **E6/5**

E6/7 General view (no scale)

E6/7

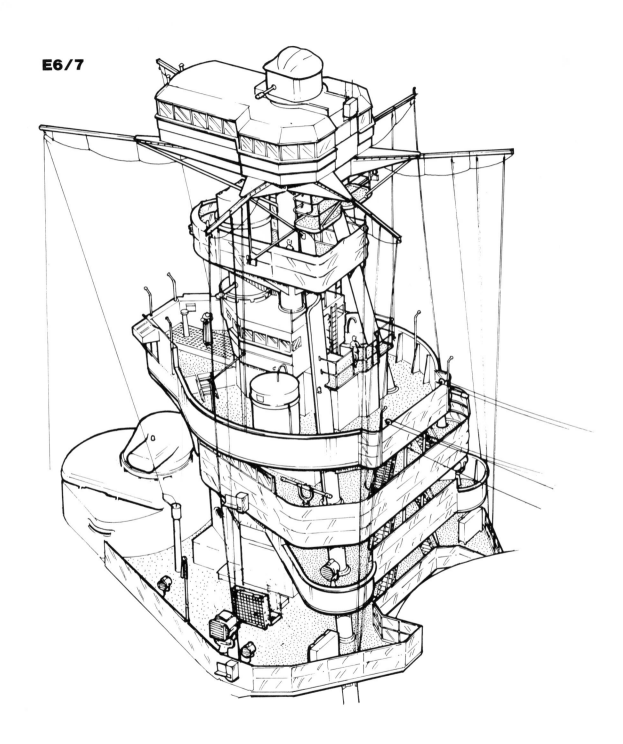

E7/1

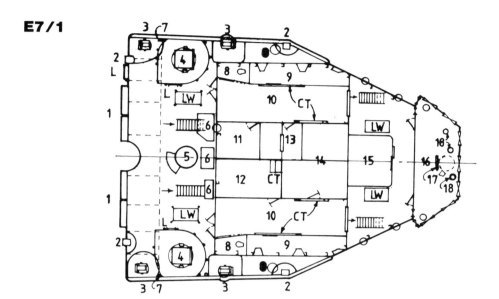

E7/2

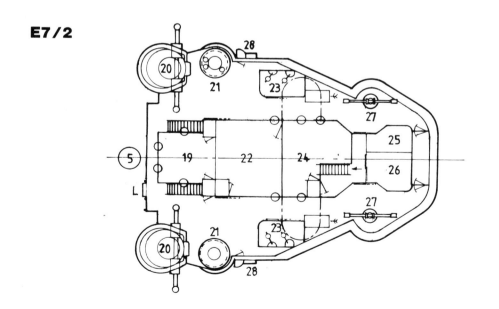

E Superstructure

E7/3

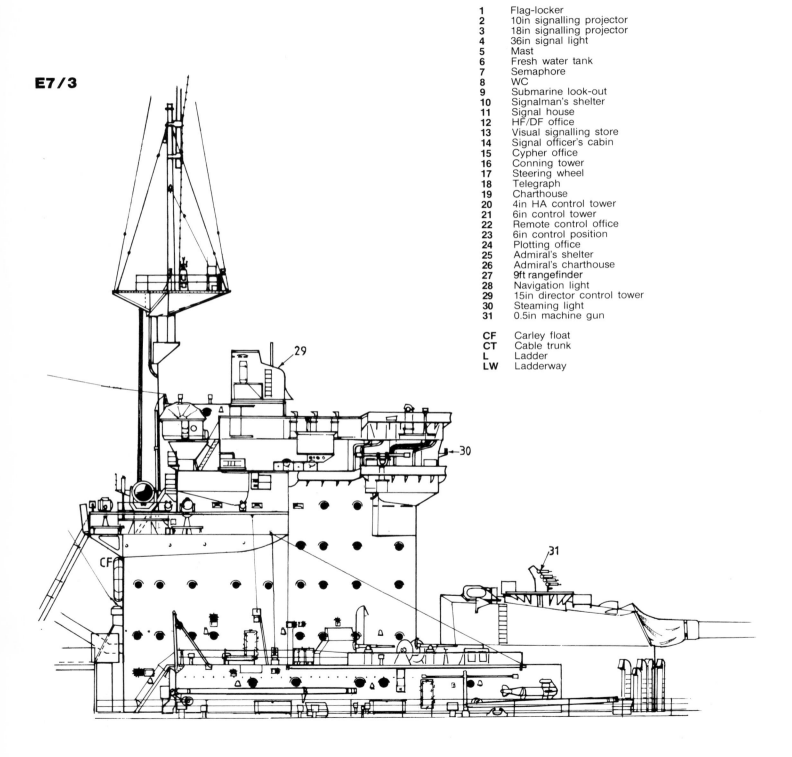

E7/3 Profile

1	Flag-locker
2	10in signalling projector
3	18in signalling projector
4	36in signal light
5	Mast
6	Fresh water tank
7	Semaphore
8	WC
9	Submarine look-out
10	Signalman's shelter
11	Signal house
12	HF/DF office
13	Visual signalling store
14	Signal officer's cabin
15	Cypher office
16	Conning tower
17	Steering wheel
18	Telegraph
19	Charthouse
20	4in HA control tower
21	6in control tower
22	Remote control office
23	6in control position
24	Plotting office
25	Admiral's shelter
26	Admiral's charthouse
27	9ft rangefinder
28	Navigation light
29	15in director control tower
30	Steaming light
31	0.5in machine gun

CF	Carley float
CT	Cable trunk
L	Ladder
LW	Ladderway

E8

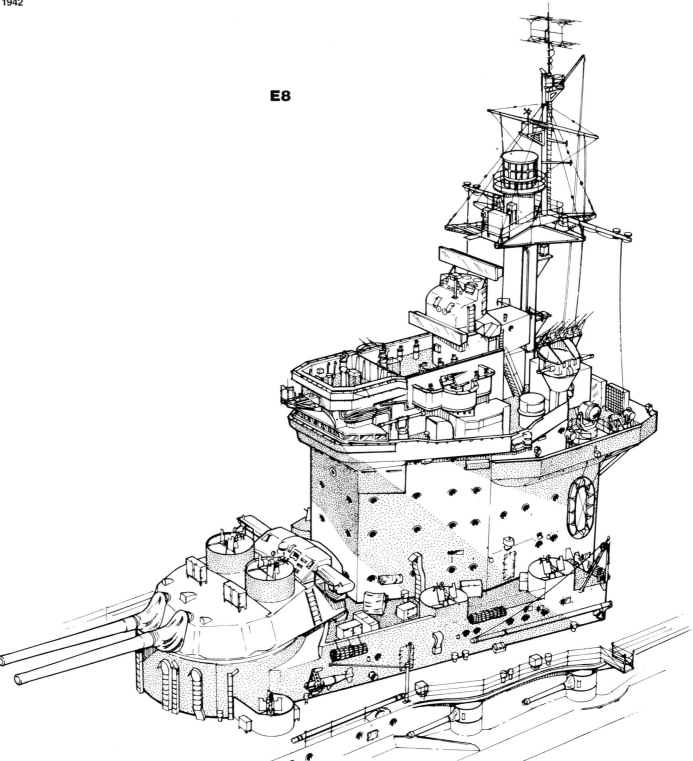

F Rig

F1 MAIN DERRICK (1/200 scale)

1 Topping lift
2 Purchase wire
3 Leading block
4 Single leading blocks
5 Double block
6 Purchase
7 Securing guys
8 Working guys
9 Sheave
10 Section through derrick
11 Hoop for standing lift

F2 RIG TO FOREMAST (1/200 scale)

F2/1 Profile 1917

F2/2 Plan 1917

F2/3 Fog siren platform (enlarged 1917)

1 Flashing lantern
2 Topmast
3 Upper signal yard
4 Halyards
5 Forestays
6 Shrouds
7 Backstay
8 Jacob's ladder
9 Lower signal yard
10 Electric steaming light
11 Oil steaming light
12 Fog siren

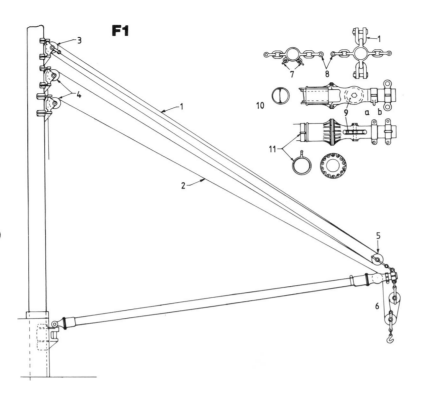

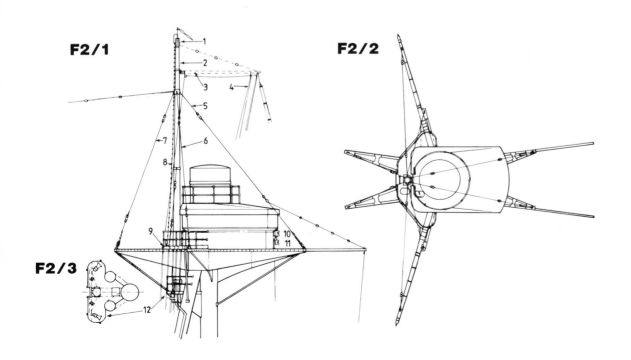

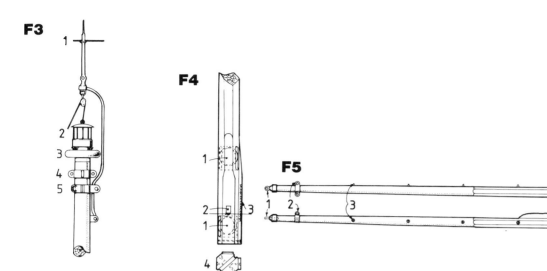

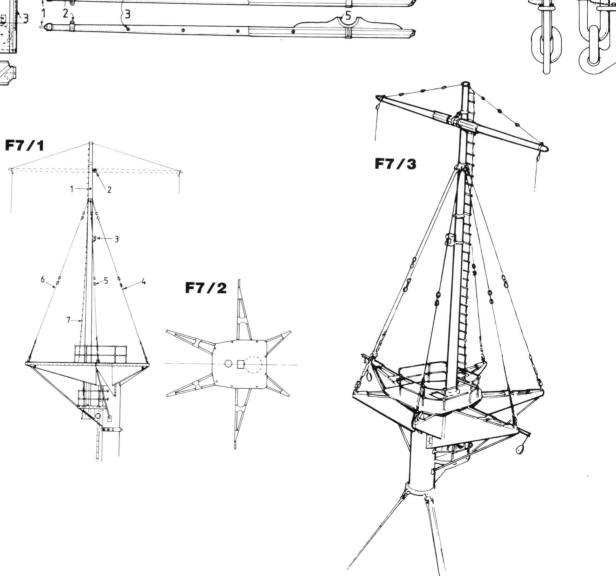

F3   **TOPMAST FLASHING LANTERN**

1   Weather vane
2   Lantern
3   Truck
4   For upper yard lifts
5   For Jacob's ladder

F4   **BOTTOM OF TOPMAST**

1   Sheave
2   Steel fid
3   Pawl rack
4   Section through sheave

F5   **SIGNAL YARD**

1   Signal halyard eye
2   Yard lift eye
3   Jackstay eyes
4   Band for sling
5   Leather

F6   **SCREW WITH SLIP** (for shrouds and stays)

F7   **RIG TO MAIN TOP MAST** (1/200 scale)

F7/1   Profile 1913

F7/2   Plan 1913

F7/3   General view 1913 (no scale)

F Rig

1   Topmast
2   Upper yardarm
3   Electric steaming light
4   Forestay
5   Shrouds
6   Backstay
7   Jacob's ladder
8   Topgallant mast
9   Flashing lantern with weather vane
10 W/T (wireless telegraphy) yard
11 Admiral's flag pole
12 Gaff
13 Lower yardarm
14 Yardarm running fore and aft
15 Helm position indicator

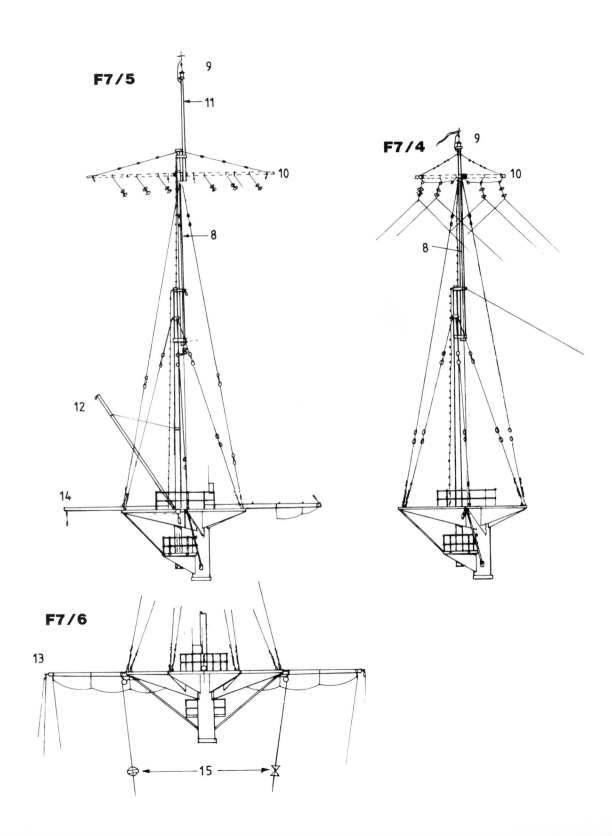

F8   FORETOP 1921 (1/200 scale)

F8/1   Profile

F8/2   Plan

F8/3   Front elevation (starboard half)

1   HA control tower
2   15in director tower
3   Wind vane
4   Anemometer
5   Steaming lights
6   Recognition lights
7   Fog siren
8   Range clocks

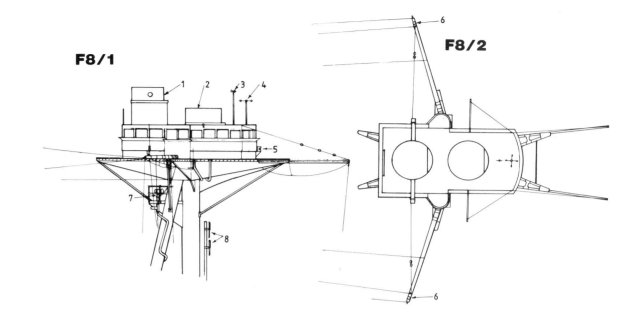

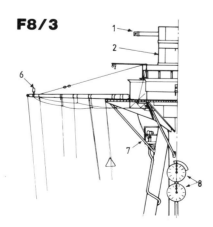

F Rig

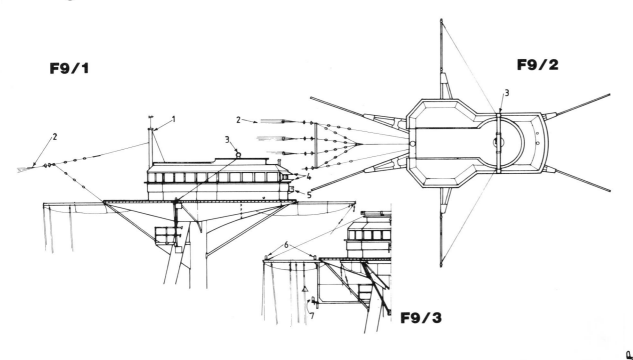

F9/1

F9/2

F9/3

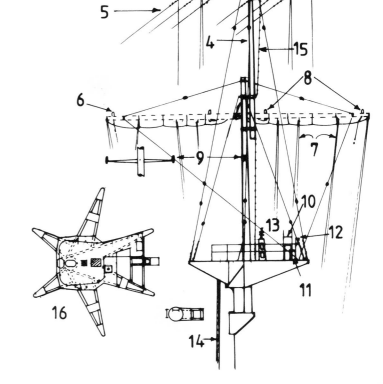

F10

F9   **FORETOP 1926 (1/200 scale)**

F9/1   **Profile**

F9/2   **Plan**

F9/3   **Front elevation (starboard half)**

1   Short stump mast
2   WT aerials
3   HA rangefinder
4   Anti-glare shield
5   Steaming light
6   Recognition lights
7   Fixed manoeuvring lights

F10   **FORE TOPMAST 1937 (1/200 scale)**

1   HF/DF coil
2   Twin masthead flashing lights
3   24ft W/T yard
4   Topgallant mast
5   Main W/T aerials
6   48ft signal yard
7   Signal halyards
8   Flashing lanterns
9   Fixed manoeuvring lights
10   Type 75 W/T unit
11   Distance reading thermograph
12   Steaming light
13   Combined wind vane and
       anemometer
14   Steel ladder
15   Jacob's ladder
16   Starfish platform

F11 **MAINMAST 1937 (1/200 scale)**

1   MF/DF (medium frequency
    direction-finding) aerials
2   DF pole
3   Mainmast platform
4   Martingale
5   Admiral's shaded toplight
6   30ft helm signal yard
7   Position lights
8   Helm signal gear
9   20ft W/T yard

F12 **FOREMAST 1942 (1/200 scale)**

1   Type 281 RDF aerial
2   'Headache' ECM device (added
    1944)
3   Gaff
4   Masthead flashing lights
5   Combined wind vane and
    anemometer
6   24ft W/T yard
7   Type 86 TBS (Talk Between Ships)
    short range radio
8   Fixed manoeuvring lights
9   Halyard spur
10 Type 273 radar lantern
11 Distance reading thermograph
12 Daylight signalling light
13 48ft signal yard
14 Type 650 jamming device
15 Flashing lights
16 Jacob's ladder
17 Topmast
18 Topmast rest
19 Type 243 IFF (Identification Friend or
    Foe) aerial (added 1944)

F13 **MAINMAST 1942**

1   Type 281 RDF (radar) aerial
2   Admiral's top light
3   Type 91 TBS (added 1943)
4   Main W/T aerials
5   Radar beacons (added 1943)
6   Helm indication
7   Type 75 W/T unit

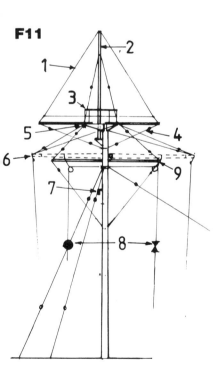

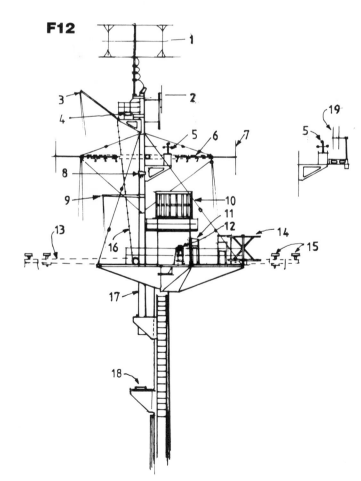

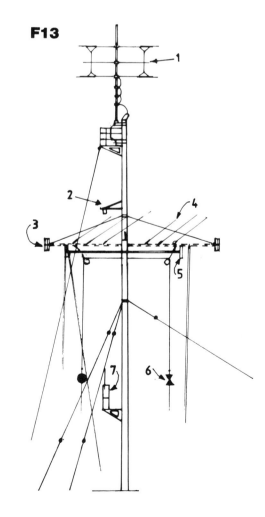

G Armament

G1   **15in Mk I MOUNTING (1/100 scale)**

G1/1   **Plan of gunhouse**

G1/2   **Profile (section at right gun well, except gunhouse armour and cabin sectioned on centre-line)**

G1/3   **Rear view section**

G1/4   **Half plan of working chamber and working chamber roof**

G1/5   **General view (no scale)**

1	Cabinet
2	Radial crane
3	Rammer engine
4	Sub-calibre gun
5	Gun loading hoist controls
6	Clutch handwheel
7	Elevation receiver
8	Trunnion bracket
9	Local trainer
10	Gun loading cage
11	Rangefinder hood
12	Auxiliary cordite hoist
13	Access to turret
14	Double walking pipes
15	Elevating cylinder
16	Training wormwheel case
17	Lifting jack
18	Turntable rollers
19	Training rack
20	Training pinion
21	Gun loading cage lifting press
22	Main hoist lifting press
23	Rammers
24	Waiting position
25	Hand/electric pump
26	Gun loading cage
27	Shell waiting tray
28	Shell bins
29	Shell grab
30	Traversing shell carrier
31	Shell in main cage
32	Secondary shell hoist
33	Training cut-off gear
34	Main walking pipes
35	Turret buffer
36	Auxiliary cordite hoist cylinder
38	Air bottle
39	Kilroy's danger signal
40	Cordite hopper
41	Spring guide rollers
42	Rack on trunk
43	Revolving shell bogie

G1/1

G1/4

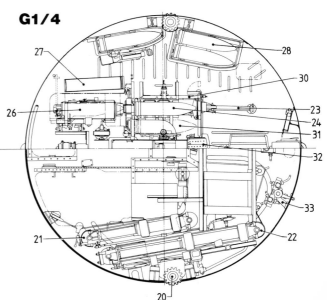

G1/5

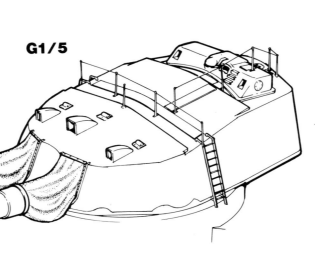

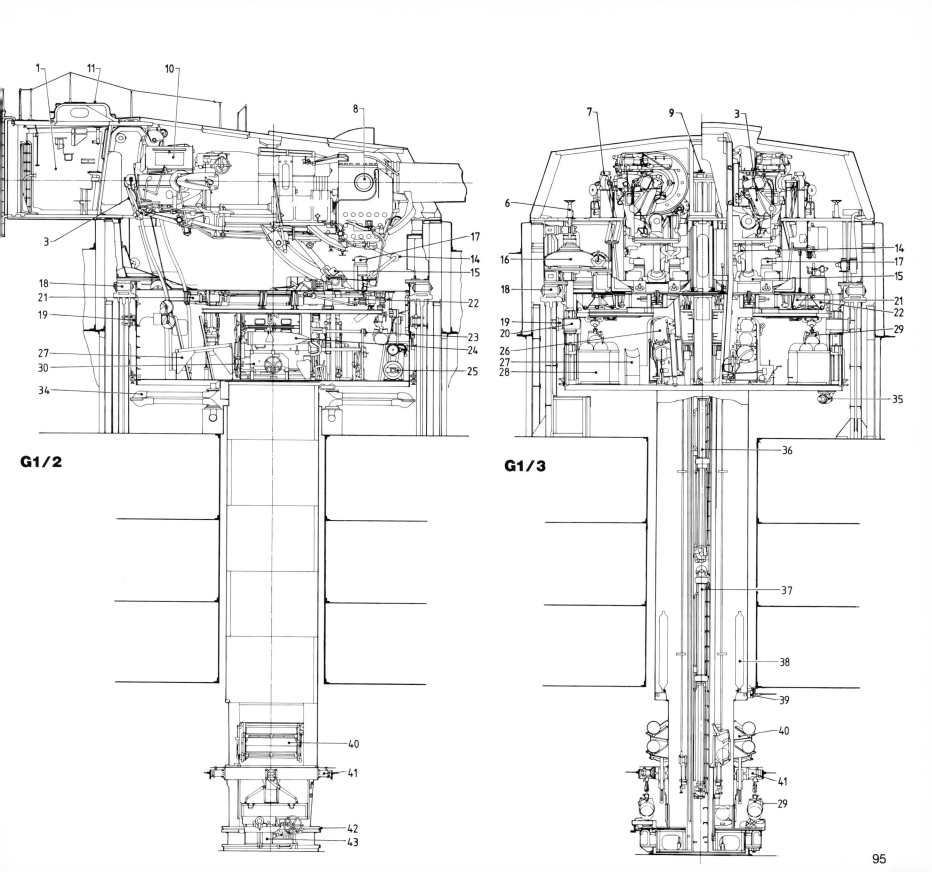

G1/2

G1/3

G Armament

G2 **15in Mk I (N) BREECH (right-hand gun; no scale)**

1 Hydraulic cylinder
2 Rack
3 Air-blast pipe
4 Carrier
5 Breech screw
6 Breech safety contact
7 Electric lock
8 Hand lever actuating lock
9 Handwheel
10 Clutch lever

G3 **15in Mk I GUN (section; 1/75 scale)**

1 Breech mechanism frame
2 Breech ring
3 Jacket
4 'A' tube
5 Inner 'A' tube
6 Wire
7 'B' tube
8 Stop ring
9 Shrunk collar
10 Breech bush

G2

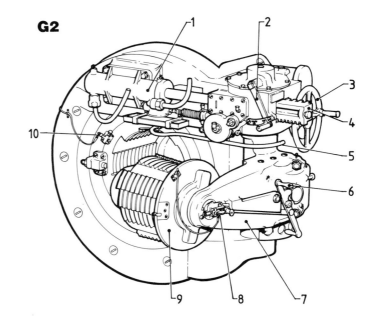

G3

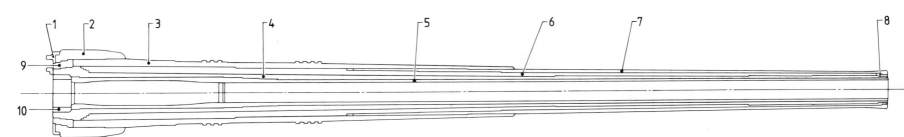

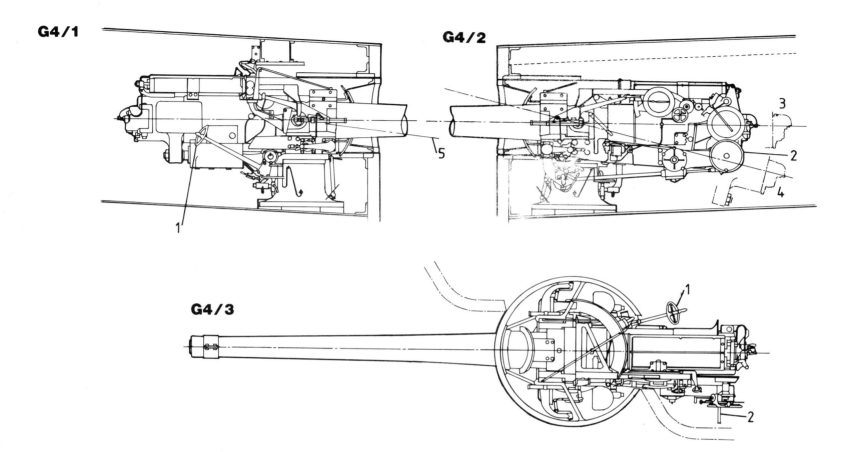

G4/1

G4/2

3

2

4

5

1

G4/3

1

2

2

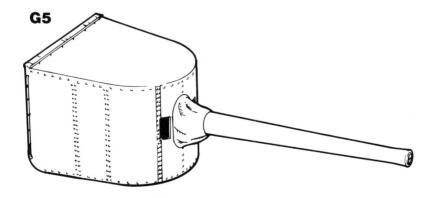

G5

G4	6in Mk XII PEDESTAL MOUNTING (1/50 scale)
G4/1	Right-hand elevation
G4/2	Left-hand elevation
G4/3	Plan
1	Training handwheel
2	Elevating handwheel
3	Working recoil
4	Maximum elevation
5	Maximum depression
G5	6in Mk XII GUN IN OPEN MOUNTING (general view; no scale)

G Armament

G6   3in Mk I GUN (1/50 scale)

G6/1   Left-hand elevation

G6/2   Rear view elevation

G6/3   Plan

1   Training handwheel
2   Elevating handwheel
3   Trainer's sight
4   Gunlayer's sight

G7   4in HA Mk III MOUNTING (1/100 scale)

1   Recuperator
2   Carriage
3   Trunnion
4   Trainer's sight
5   Training handles
6   Vertical training shaft
7   Loading tray

G6/1

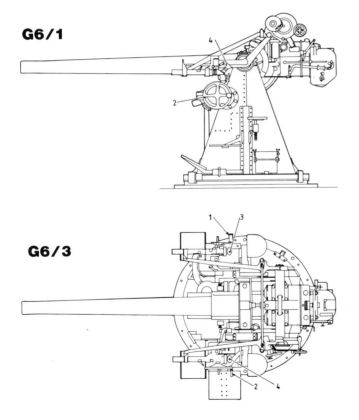

G6/2

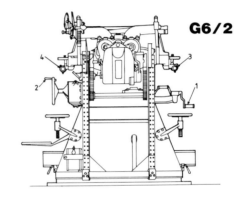

G6/3

G7

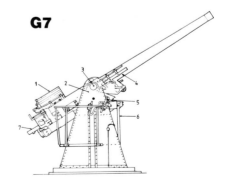

G8   4in Mk XIX MOUNTING (1/50 scale)

G8/1   Plan with shield removed

G8/2   Sectioned left-hand profile

G8/3   Rear elevation

1	Elevating receiver
2	Barrage sight
3	Aldis telescope
4	Sight arm
5	Training receiver
6	Sights
7	Training handles
8	Trainer's seat
9	Fuse-setter's seat
10	Mk II fuse-setting machine
11	Interceptor
12	Compensating tank (recoil cylinder)
13	Recuperator cylinder
14	Balance rings
15	Recuperator ram guard
16	Recuperator ram
17	Loading lamp
18	Breech mechanism
19	Hand-operated firing gear
20	Junction box
21	Layer's seat
22	Elevating handles
23	Extended sight ports
24	Safety firing gear
25	Intensifier
26	Rounds fired counter
27	Semi-automatic gear
28	Buffer stops
29	Hydraulic training buffer
30	Rollers centre pivot
31	Training pinion
32	Training rack
33	Training rollers
34	Evershed bearing
35	Starshell spirit level
36	Elevating arc
37	Housing stop
38	Training base clips

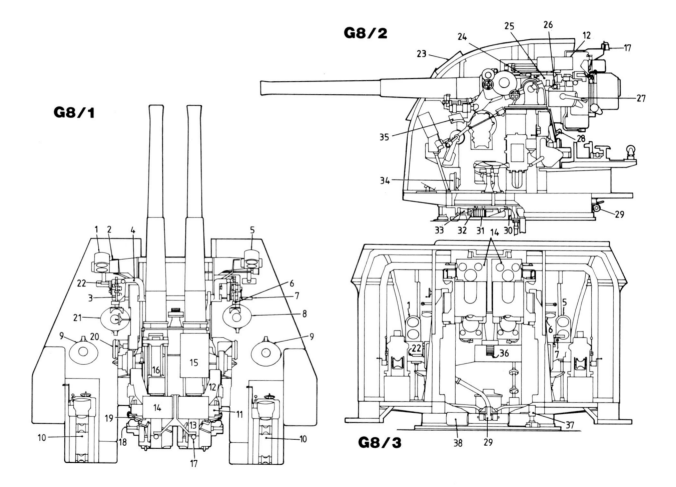

G Armament

G9 MULTIPLE Mk VIA 2pdr POM-POM MOUNTING (no scale)

1 Trainer's sight
2 Interrupter handles
3 Layer's sight
4 Cartridge divertor
5 Electric motor
6 Empty cartridge shute
7 Ammunition magazine

G10 QUADRUPLE 0.5in Mk III MOUNTING (1/25 scale)

G10/1 Profile

G10/2 Rear elevation

1 Layer's open sight
2 Trainer's open sight
3 Elevating arc
4 Elevating handwheel
5 Layer's body rest
6 Elevating worm gear box
7 Housing stop
8 Safety depression control roller and link
9 Trainer's firing lever
10 Ammunition drums
11 Training handwheel

G11 20mm TWIN Mk V OERLIKON MOUNTING (1/25 scale)

G11/1 Profile

G11/2 Plan

1 Cartwheel foresight
2 Sight link
3 Magazine
4 Firing rod
5 Firing can
6 Fire interruptor operating lever
7 Layer's seat
8 Firing valve
9 Elevating valve
10 Control handle
11 Training motor
12 Cocking lever

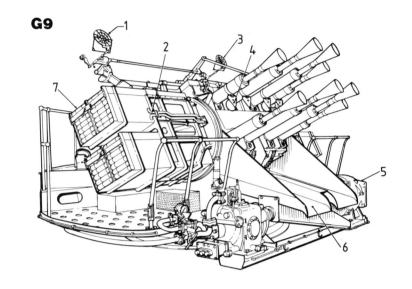

G9

G11/1

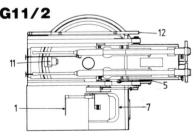

G11/2

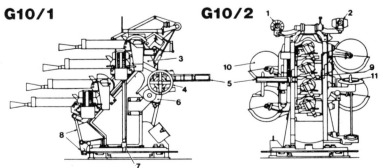

G10/1

G10/2

G12   20mm SINGLE Mk IV OERLIKON ON PEDESTAL MOUNTING (1/25 scale)

G13   3pdr SALUTING GUN (1/25 scale)

G14   SUBMERGED TORPEDO ROOM (1/200 scale)

1   Torpedo tube
2   21in torpedo
3   Firing reservoirs
4   Tanks
5   Air reservoirs
6   Exercise heads
7   Drain pocket
8   Work bench
9   Cupboards
10 Runway (over)

G12

G13

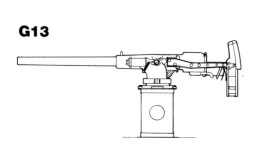

G14

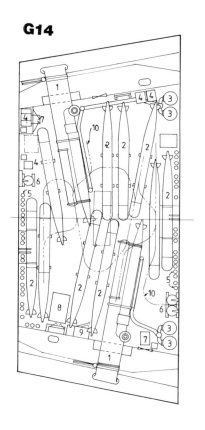

H Fire control

H1 SPOTTING TOP 1915 (1/100 scale)

H1/1 Profile
1 15in gun director tower
2 Manhole
3 Ladder
4 Rangefinder
5 Wood gratings
6 Mast and entrance

H1/2 General view

H2 15in GUN CONTROL TOWER (1/100 scale)

1 Armoured director
2 Conning tower
3 Rangefinder
4 Tripod-type director
5 Look-out sights
6 Steering wheel
7 Armoured door

H1/1

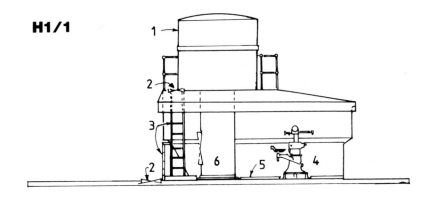

H1/2

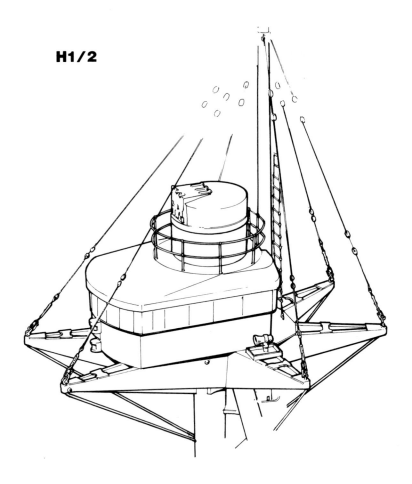

H2

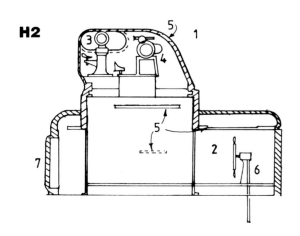

H3 **15in DIRECTOR CONTROL TOWER**
ADDED IN 1934 (1/100 scale)

H3/1 **Profile**

H3/2 **Front elevation**

H3/3 **Plan**

1 Dial sight Type GB2
2 15ft rangefinder
3 Rear windows
4 Control officer's look-out
5 Rate officer's look-out
6 Spotting officer's look-out
7 Inclinometer look-out
8 Kent clear view screen, for gyro
director sight

H3/1

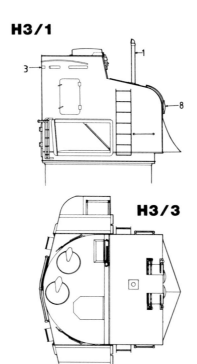

H3/2

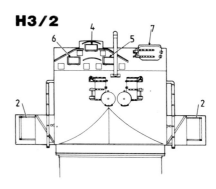

H3/3

I Fittings

I1 STERNWALK (1/200 scale)

I1/1 Plan of canopy

I1/2 Starboard profile

I2 TYPICAL WATER-TIGHT DOOR

1 Clip
2 Hinge
3 Handle

I3 TYPICAL SKYLIGHT

1 Stanchion
2 Lug for stanchion
3 Frosted glass
4 Hinged window frame
5 Butterfly clips
6 Hinge

I4 TYPICAL HATCH

1 Clips
2 Hinge
3 Rubber seal

I5 TYPICAL 'MUSHROOM' VENTS

1 Mesh opening
2 Operating handwheel

I6 TYPICAL ENGINE ROOM VENT

I7 FOG SIREN

1 Training pulley
2 Operating lever
3 Steam inlet

I8 BOLLARDS

I1/1

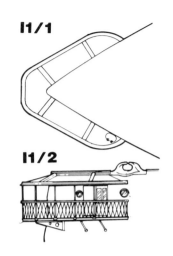

I1/2

I5

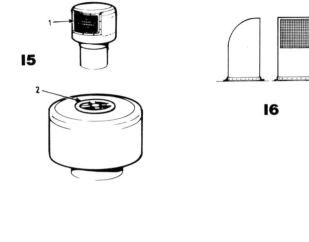

I6

I7

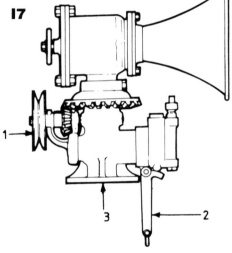

I3

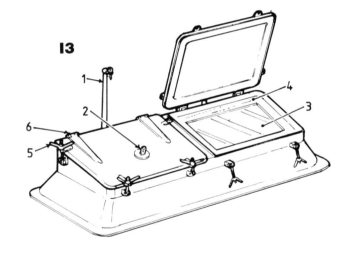

I2

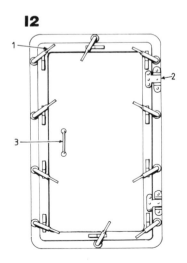

I4

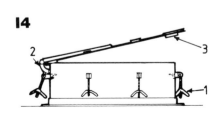

I8

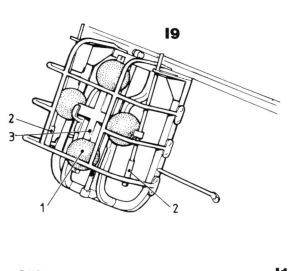

I9

I10

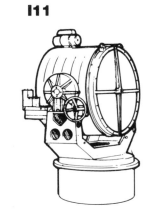

I11

I9	NIGHT LIFEBUOY
1	Copper floats
2	Calcium light tubes
3	Wood cross
I10	40in SEARCHLIGHT
I11	44in SEARCHLIGHT
I12	36in SEARCHLIGHT
I13	20in SIGNAL LAMP
I14	10in SIGNAL LAMP
I15	FLOTANET (stowed position)
I16	QUARTERDECK CAPSTAN
I17	4in READY-USE LOCKER (1934)

I12

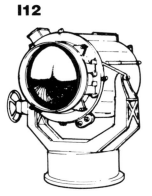

I13

I14

I17

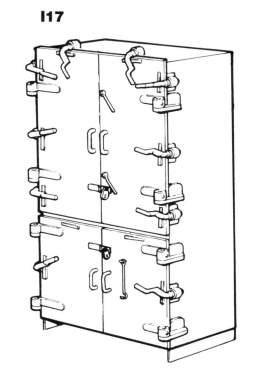

I15

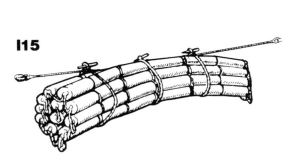

I16

▌ Fittings

I18   **WASH DECK LOCKER**

I19   **SIGNAL LOCKER**

I18

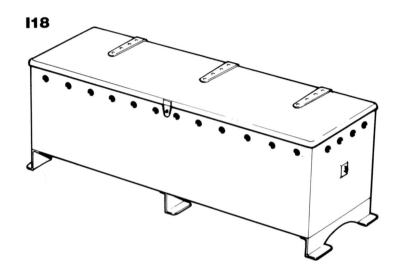

I19

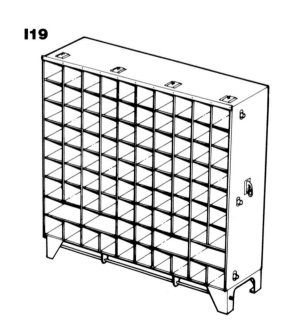

I20   DISRUPTIVE CAMOUFLAGE (1/900 scale; see also back jacket illustration)

I20/1   Port profile (1942)

I20/2   Starboard profile (1942)

I20/3   Port profile (1943)

1   Medium grey
2   Light grey

I20/1

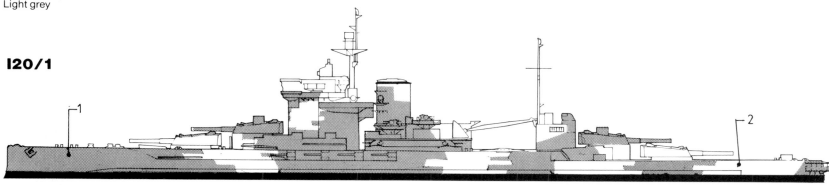

I20/2

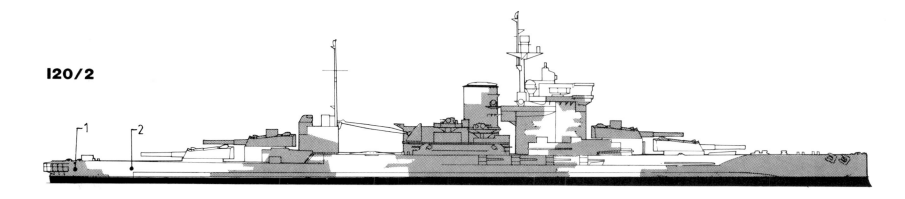

I20/3

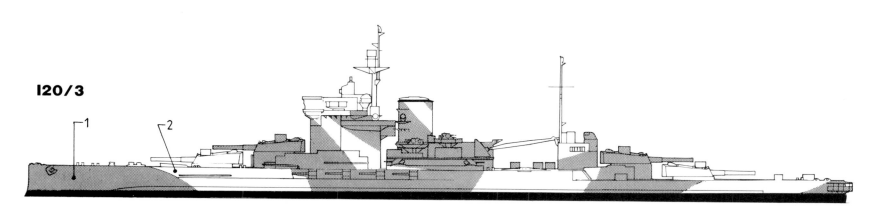

J Ground tackle

J1   **FORWARD CAPSTAN GEAR (1/50 scale)**

J1/1   **Capstan for bower cable (sectional elevation and plan)**

1   Brake handwheel
2   Bevel pinion
3   Drum
4   Spindle
5   Brake band
6   Fulcrum pin
7   Driving disc

J1/2   **Capstan for sheet cable (sectional elevation)**

J1/3   **Middle line capstan (sectional elevation and plan)**

1   Roller
2   Capstan bar shoe
3   Portable double whelp
4   Spindle

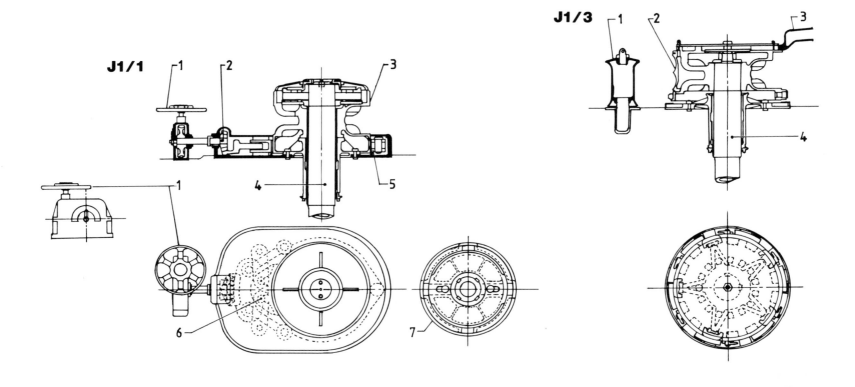

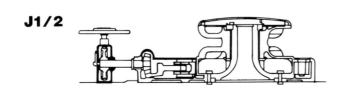

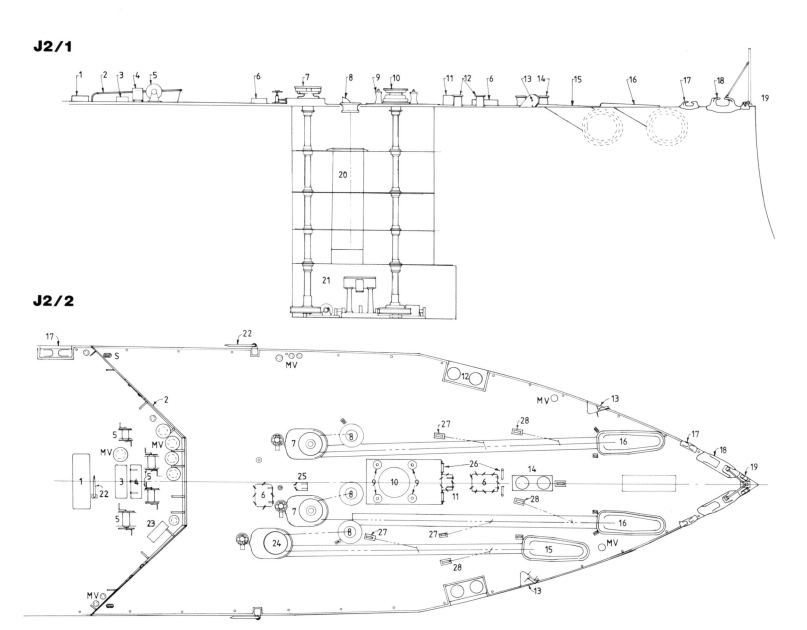

J2 ARRANGEMENT OF ANCHORS AND CABLES ON FORECASTLE DECK (1/200 scale)

J2/1 Profile

J2/2 Plan

1	Torpedo hatch
2	Breakwater
3	Sickbay skylight
4	Wash deck locker
5	Reel
6	Ladderway
7	Cable holder
8	Deck pipe
9	Rollers
10	Capstan
11	Vent to capstan engine room
12	Bollards
13	Clump cathead
14	Centre-line bollard
15	Sheet anchor hawsepipe
16	Bower anchor hawsepipe
17	Hawser fairlead
18	Towing fairlead
19	Paravane fairlead
20	Cable locker
21	Capstan engine room
22	Davit
23	Cable gear
24	Sheet anchor cable holder
25	Exhaust to capstan engine room
27	Brake slip
28	Bottle screw slip

J2/1

J2/2

J Ground tackle

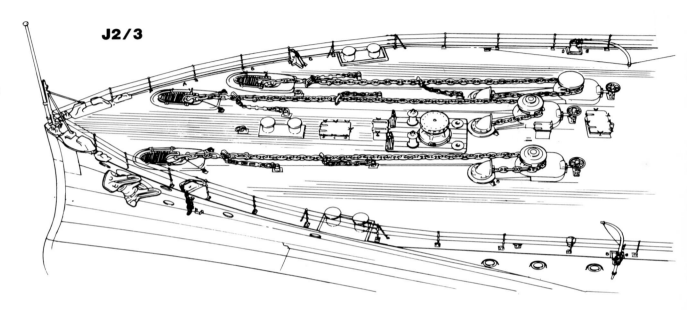

J2/3

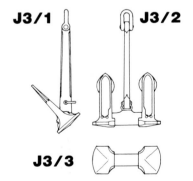

J3/1   **J3/2**

J3/3

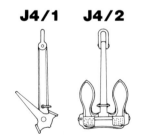

J4/1   **J4/2**

J5/1   **J5/2**

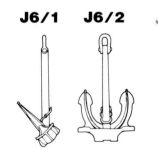

J6/1   **J6/2**

K Boats

K1 **SECTION AT RADIAL DAVIT**
(1/50 scale)

1 Bottle screw slip
2 Metal blocks
3 Wood blocks
4 Fairlead
5 Griping spar
6 Griping band
7 Jackstay
8 Jacob's ladder
9 Cleat
10 Hinged seating

K2 **32ft CUTTER ON RADIAL DAVITS**
(no scale)

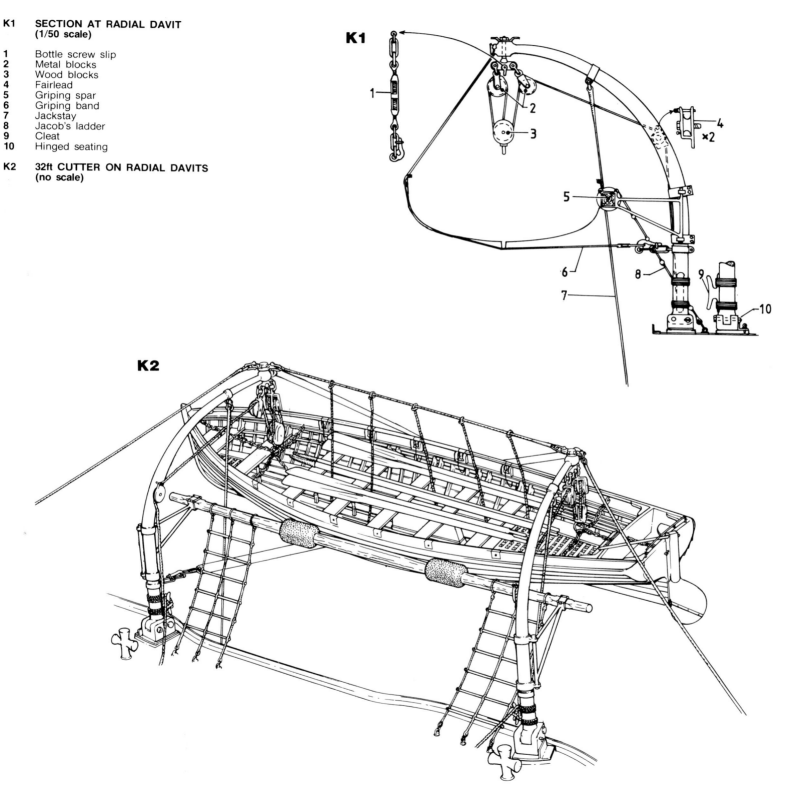

K Boats

K3   50ft **STEAM PINNACE** (no scale)

K4   45ft **ADMIRAL'S BARGE** (no scale)

K3

K4

K5

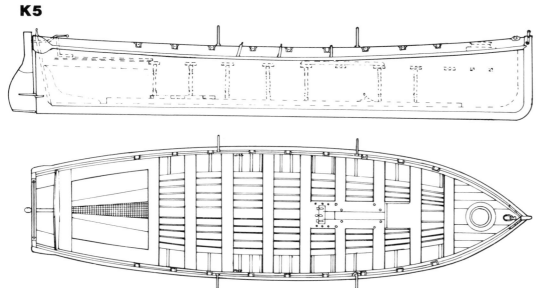

K6

K7

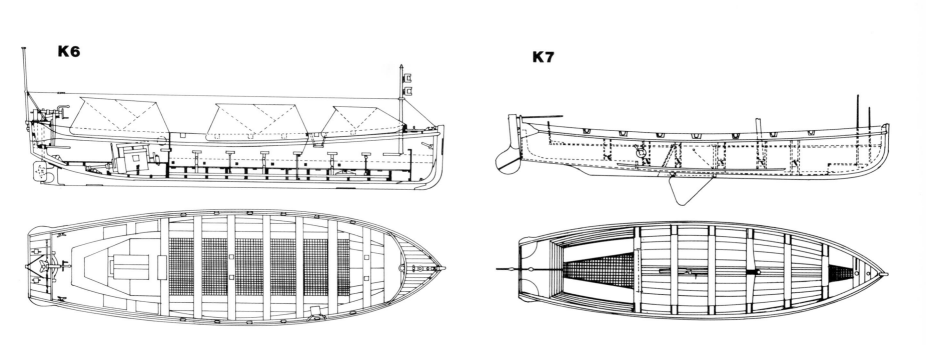

K Boats

K8   30ft GIG

K9   27ft WHALER

K10 16ft DINGHY

K8

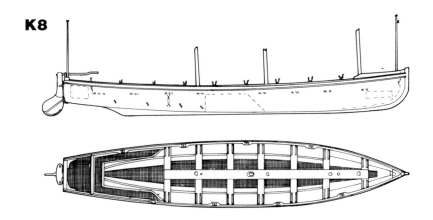

K9

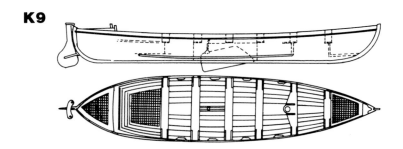

K10

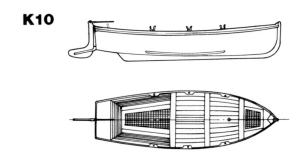

K11

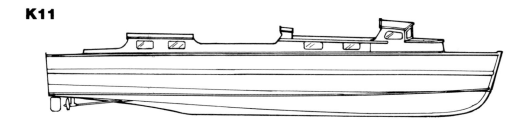

K12

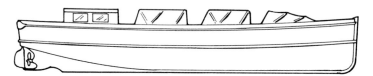

K13

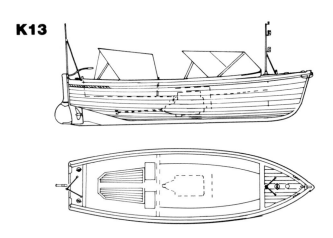

L1 SOPWITH 2F1 CAMEL (L1–L5 1/100 scale)

L2 SOPWITH 1½-STRUTTER

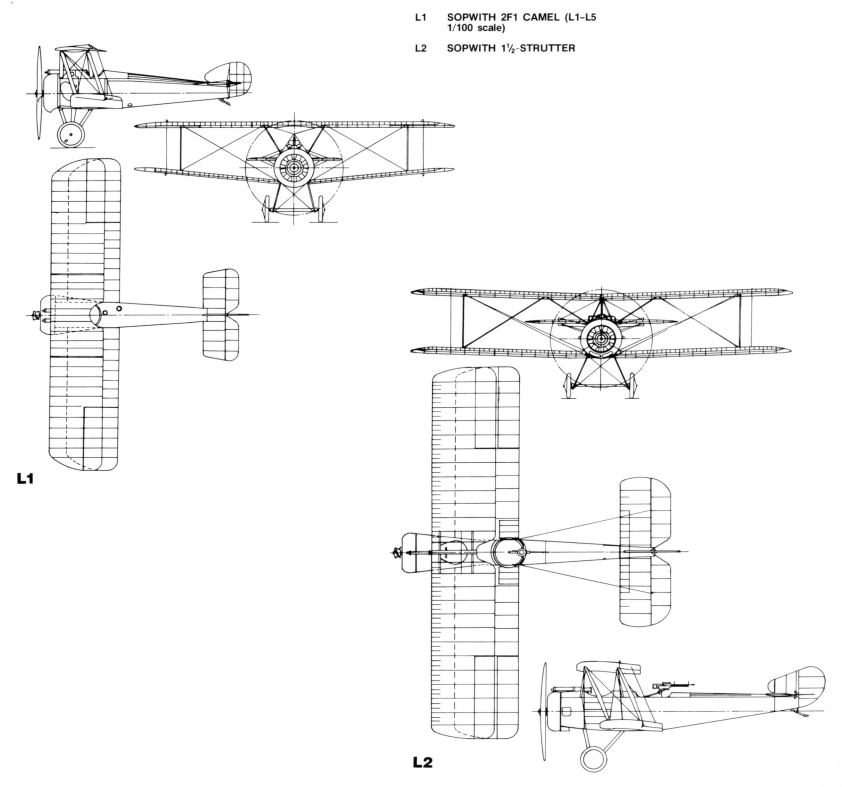

L1

L2

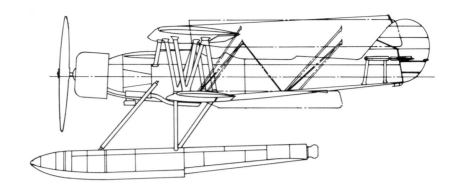

L3

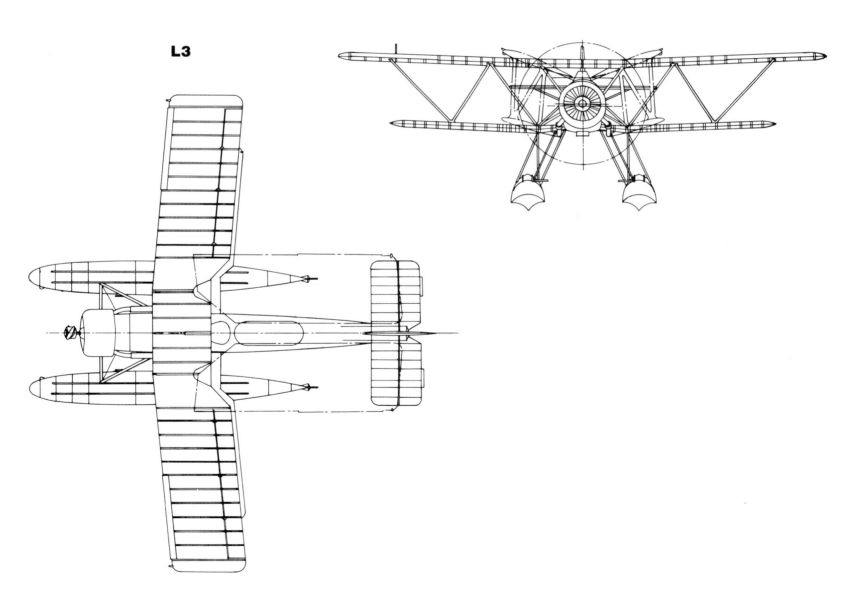

L4   **FAIREY SWORDFISH Mk I**

L4

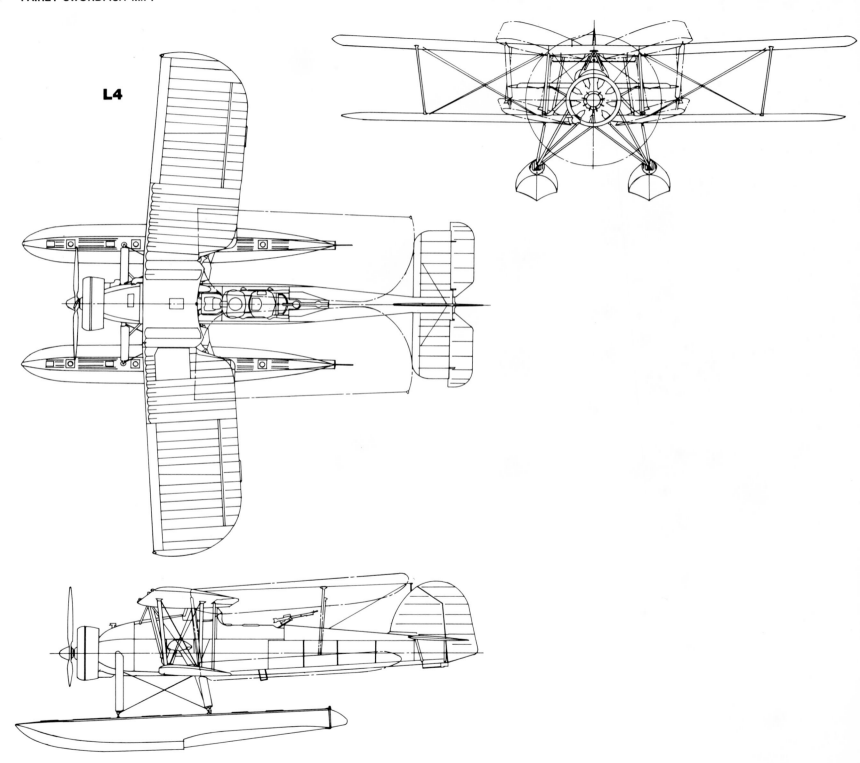

L5

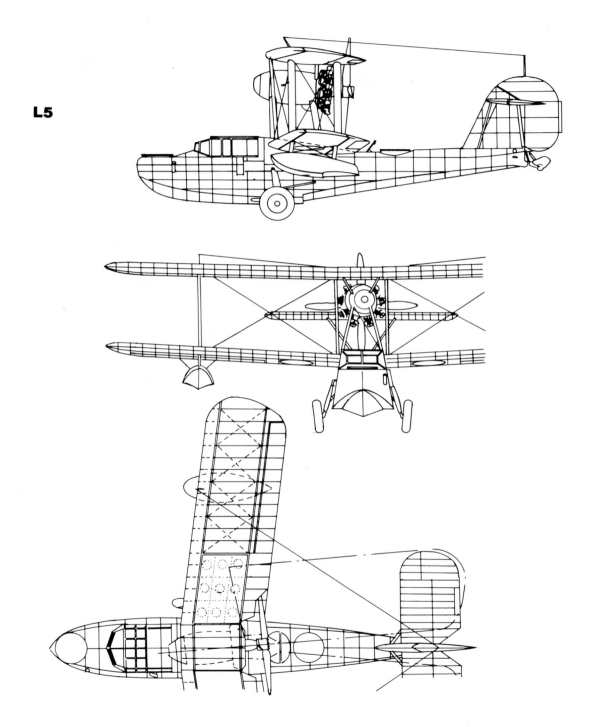

L Aircraft arrangements

L6 GENERAL VIEW OF THE
SOPWITH 1½-STRUTTER AND
FLYING-OFF PLATFORM ON 'B'
TURRET (no scale)

L6

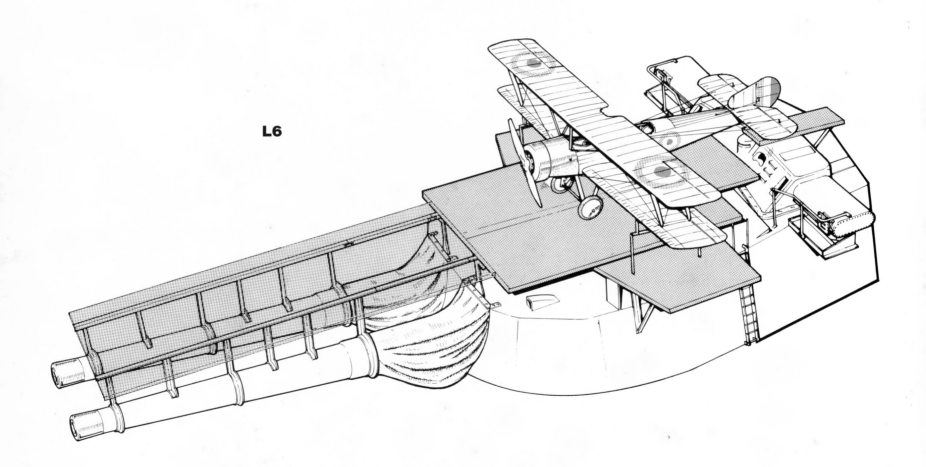